The Rabbi's Daughter

The Rabbi's Daughter

A Novel

Alan Sorem

RESOURCE *Publications* • Eugene, Oregon

THE RABBI'S DAUGHTER

Resource Publications
An Imprint of Wipf and Stock Publishers
199 W. 8th Ave., Suite 3
Eugene, OR 97401

www.wipfandstock.com

ISBN 13: 978-1-4982-1843-6   02/05/2015

Manufactured in the U.S.A.

Surely the Lord is my salvation. Therefore I will trust, and will not be afraid, for the Lord is my strength and my might . . .
Isaiah 12:2a

Fides et Fortis

Prologue

It was a frigid Wednesday morning in Boston.

The telephone rang in the other room. Loudly, reminding the old man that he had increased the volume and number of rings to maximum to give him time to reach the phone before the message machine kicked in.

He lay the morning *Globe* on the breakfast table, picked up his coffee cup, pushed down on the table with his left hand and rose slowly from the chair.

Everything was slower lately. Even his morning pills seemed to take longer to kick in.

He shuffled into the living room and picked up the handset after the eleventh ring. His granddaughter Sigrid was always after him to get one of the newfangled wireless phones he could carry around in his pocket, but he was old-fashioned.

"Frank, I hope I didn't wake you."

The old man looked at his watch. A little past seven.

"No, no. I'm always up by now."

He recognized the voice. It was Tom, one of his prize Ph.D. students years ago. Now in his fifties, he was the head of The Ephesus Project in Turkey. Frank had written a glowing reference letter to the committee that subsequently appointed Tom.

"How are things in Boston?"

"The Celtics won last night, we had ten inches of snow, and I'm wondering if the taxi can get through to pick me up for my doctor's appointment at one."

"I heard you're having some medical issues."

"Yes. I'm still kicking, just not as high. But you're not calling from Turkey to inquire about my health."

A laugh came down the line. "Right. I have some news and wanted to check in with you." The excitement in Tom's voice was palpable.

"Go ahead."

"I'm on a secure line at the embassy in Ankara. I'll be brief."

"Something turn up?"

The words were emphatic. "Yes, two scrolls. In a secure hiding place in the cellar wall of the ruins of the house of a high official."

"Age?"

"Incredible. Had a German lab test it with the smallest sample of both. Authenticated yesterday on an encrypted line at the Embassy in Ankara. We have the larger scroll in a helium wrap. In a secure chamber we unwrapped and unrolled the smaller one and sealed it in the special frame."

"And?" He took a sip of coffee.

"Hold on a sec. Let me close the door."

He heard footsteps going and returning.

"You there, Frank?"

"Yes."

"Sorry, can't be too careful with something of this magnitude in dating."

"How much magnitude?"

"More than I ever would have dreamed possible."

Frank took another sip of coffee. "Early?"

"Let me put it this way. You know the date of the Codex Sinaiticus."

Frank thought for a moment. The earliest discovered complete New Testament in Greek.

"Of course. Middle of the fourth century."

"Now think of the Gospel of Mark."

"Well, there's the P45 fragment, possibly two fifty. Earliest we have."

"Until now."

"Oh?"

"Yes. Think maybe a hundred fifty years earlier. Plus a couple of decades."

"You're pulling my leg."

"No."

"Is this April First? You've got to be kidding!"

The man on the other end laughed. "I'm not kidding."

"You have a fragment from the nineties?"

"Earlier. In the mid-sixties. Nero was emperor."

"No such thing exists!"

"It does now. And much more than a fragment."

"You say the German lab confirmed?"

"Dating? Absolutely. They're not aware of what's on the scroll."

The telephone line was silent except for humming.

"Tom?"

Tom's voice was a whisper. "What we've always hoped for. A golden find like the Isaiah scroll you worked on from Qumran."

The old man put his coffee cup down. The earliest Gospel of Mark by far. Dear God! He cleared his throat.

"How much do you have?"

"Too early to tell. We only unwrapped the very first part. We want the rest to be done very, very slowly. But the thickness of the wrap indicates a complete scroll."

Frank sank into a wing chair by the side table of the telephone. It took him a moment to reply.

"Tom, be careful. Remember what the Dead Sea scrolls stirred up."

"I—we—are being very careful. But I want you to see a facsimile of the very first part. What we have of it is clear. Good penmanship in Greek. Large lettering. Looks like it was meant to be read aloud."

"Lussier's hypothesis. Whole gospel to be read serially during Holy Week."

"Yes. What I want to do is send you a copy of the first part by overnight express. See what you think."

Frank sighed. "I don't know that I can help. I'm spending a lot of time with doctors and my eyesight's not so good."

"But this is the big one. I value your opinion, as ever. And you've had experience with how to break the news. Please."

"All right. I'll do what I can. No others involved."

"Thanks, Frank. Oh, and I'll also send a full copy of the smaller scroll that was inside the same sealed large jar. It may be dynamite also."

"Something biblical?"

"No. Burial instructions for a woman in the early church community in Ephesus. It mentions two daughters, Elizabeth and Rebecca. The woman asks that the burial instructions be kept at the house of the Ephesus church's Chief Elder. And get this: she says the instructions are to be kept with the account by Mark. Different handwriting at the end: 'I sign this with my own hand. The Rabbi's Daughter, M.'"

"Burial instructions? For a woman? That's odd."

"Obviously a woman of importance."

"And together with the other scroll, you say."

"Yes," answered Tom. "The Greek characters of the last part are shaky. An old woman."

"An important elderly woman in Ephesus."

"Yes. I may be jumping to conclusions, but—oh, never mind."

"What?"

"The letter 'M.'"

There was a long pause. At last he asked, "The dating is the same?"

"Yes."

"But surely she died years before."

"I know. She would have had to be seventy-five or older."

"Tom, these two finds are incredible!"

"That's why I want you to take a look. I'll send the facsimiles by overnight express. We're six hours ahead of you. If Logan Airport is open you should get the packet by tomorrow afternoon."

"This is amazing! Possibly two monumental discoveries in first century documents!"

On the other end of the line, Tom laughed.

"You got it! I'm in Ankara for a couple of days. I'll call you on Friday to make sure the package has arrived. Is that okay?"

"Sure. Try to get me around this same time. I have two medical appointments on Friday."

"Will do. And Frank, one more thing. Thank you for all that you taught me."

"My pleasure."

"Bye now."

"Bye."

The elderly man's hands were shaking from so much excitement that it took him three attempts before he could replace the handset in its cradle.

Outside his house the winter clouds shifted and suddenly bright morning sunlight shone through his living room windows. He sat in the chair for a long time, musing as he watched the sunbeam slowly move across the room.

A Gospel of Mark fragment or perhaps the full gospel from the first century! And possibly a note signed by Mary, Mother of Jesus!

ONE

THE OLD WOMAN'S GNARLED fingers grasped at the weeds along the edge of her vegetable garden. She muttered to herself, as she always did, "Time for younger fingers to do this work."

But she never asked for help. Weeding beneath a warm springtime sun was one of the few pleasures she had after the chill of winter.

She glanced toward the foot of the long garden. Yes, she could almost make out the form of old Lazarus sitting in the worn wooden chair that once had been her husband's. Lazarus had sat there often before he went to Cyprus to escape rumored plots on his life. When the guardians rode up from the city to tell him he must go, he had laughed, a great hearty roar. But he had heeded their warnings in the end. He was proof, after all, of a second life that could not be denied.

"Mary, Mary," he gently chided now in her remembrance of his ways. "If it is more burden than pleasure, my nephew from down the hill can help. Or one of the young maidens from The Community in Ephesus."

He paused for a moment and then chuckled. "You would be doing the young maiden a favor. She would have such a tale to tell." He paused and peered about to see if other ears were listening. "Helping the Rabbi's Daughter."

She sighed. Still, after all the years, the code name used for her that began the day she was hurried away by John, one of her son's disciples, from the tragic carnival atmosphere on the hill. The terrible day of suffering and death with words of mockery flung about along with the cries of the hucksters and the vendors. The final sight as she looked back to her dying son was of the six men on horseback surveying the crowd, their calculating eyes watching for signs of resistance to the cruel execution. And one of the horsemen, the Chief Priest's man, kept his eyes always on her.

"Don't look back," John had murmured as he pulled her forward. "Don't look back."

She shook her head to rid herself of the awful memory and concentrated on the next weed in the garden.

The vegetables were sustenance for her and her daughter through the autumn, and the garden flowers, placed in a large vase from Nazareth in her simple bedroom, brought memories of her early days. The garden in Cana, lovingly tended by her mother and herself. The garden where her life had changed abruptly.

"Mary," called the Lazarus of her memory, his form growing dimmer as the sun rose. "You have a doleful countenance today."

Yes, she did. Yesterday the message had come from the head of The Community in Ephesus that she was to have a visit today with two travelers returning from the North on their way to Antioch. They were on a special mission from Simon Peter that involved her son. What could it be? Simon Peter had been crucified in Rome a year ago. On the tenth anniversary of Nero's accession to Emperor.

Two

ADAM AND BENJAMIN CAME running up the hill as only young children can run. "Grandmother, Grandmother, men are coming!"

She rose from the garden and called to Elizabeth inside the house. "Our visitors are arriving."

Elizabeth appeared at the doorway, wiping her hands on her apron.

"Yes, yes, Mama. All is prepared."

The two youngsters circled Mary, excited with their news.

"Papa is keeping their horses by the gate to give us time to come tell you." Benjamin exclaimed.

"There are three of them," stated Adam.

"Two are simply dressed," continued Benjamin.

"The other has a fine cloak," shouted Adam.

"And a sword this long!" Benjamin stretched his arms out wide.

Mary peered down the path. "They're walking up. I'll go wash my hands and put on my apron. Now, calm down, you two."

She made her way toward her small house as the boys ran back down the path to greet the three men.

Mary, wearing a new apron, was standing outside the door alongside Elizabeth as the trio approached. The two plainly dressed men stopped into the clearing and bowed to Mary. The swordsman wore a military cloak. He gave Elizabeth a smile and a nod. His eyes turned to survey the area surrounding the cottage.

"Shalom," said the younger of the two men. He then addressed Mary in the old tongue.

"Mistress, we are grateful for your kindness in receiving us. Shall we speak in the old language or in Greek?"

She realized she was staring at the other man. He closely resembled her second son, James, who had died in Jerusalem five years before.

She responded in Greek to the older man. "Forgive my rudeness. You bear the likeness of one of my sons."

"I am honored. I knew your son James in the early days. I regret his death."

He bowed. "I am Barnabas." He gestured to his companion. "Mark. I am his cousin and scribe." His cousin bowed again. "And our watchful guardian from the Chief Elder's household is Felix."

The swordsman gave Mary a nod and his gaze returned to an inspection of the surrounding woods.

"Why is a guardian needed?" Mary asked.

"These are troubled times," Mark answered.

Mary gestured toward the doorway. "My daughter Elizabeth. Please come in. Elizabeth has prepared refreshments for us."

"Thank you," Mark replied as they walked to the house. "Felix prefers to wait outside to prevent interruption by unwanted visitors."

Her grandsons had edged closer to Felix. He smiled at them and drew his sword from its scabbard and displayed it to them.

"Adam. Benjamin. That's enough. Back to your father now!" Mary clapped her hands and they ran off, Benjamin almost tripping as he turned for a last look at Felix. The swordsman laughed and gave him a fierce look before he sheathed his sword.

Bread, cheese, and fruit were set on the long table. Elizabeth offered a bowl of water and a towel for the two men to wash their hands.

They sat on benches by the table and exchanged pleasantries for a period deemed long enough by Mary.

"We rarely have visitors nowadays," she noted. "I am not clear as to why you have chosen to visit me."

Mark began. "Holy Mother—"

"Please." Mary held up a hand. "I have no use for such titles. I said as much to Paul when he visited years ago." She snorted. "Strange little man. He was so sure of himself when he persecuted apostates. And then so sure of himself when he preached and taught the Way."

"He was transformed by your son," protested Barnabas. "And the change was sincere, as we can attest. We both have traveled with him."

"Paul had his own time in the wilderness," Mark added mildly, watching Mary. "Much longer than your son Jesus did."

Mary raised her hand again. "Enough. Tell me why you wish to see me."

Mark responded. "Mistress, we are returning to Antioch soon. We stay a short while in Ephesus. We simply wish to pay our respects."

"Fine words. The Chief Elder in The Community here sent news of your coming. I sense there is more to this matter than paying respects."

Mark and Barnabas exchanged glances.

"Oh, come, come," Mary exclaimed. "I am near my eightieth year. If all we are to do is bandy words about, you may see me in my grave before all is done." She turned to her daughter. "Elizabeth, fetch the wine and cups. Perhaps the drink will loosen their tongues."

Mark chuckled as Elizabeth brought the ewer and poured from it into three cups.

"You have a reputation in The Community for frankness. I am glad to see it is true."

"Too frank by far. That is why it was arranged for me to live here."

"Mama!" Elizabeth exclaimed.

"Daughter, it was before you came." Mary turned back to the men. "Now, speak to me plainly."

"Very well," Mark replied. "You know of Peter's death?"

"Ah, Peter. Simon by birth name. Strong as an ox from pulling the nets on the Sea of Galilee. Peter the rock, my son renamed him

in Greek. He had a hearty laugh, as I remember. A man of strong
passions but possessed neither of courage or a great mind."

"Mistress, I must protest! His faith was firm to the end, crucified by soldiers on Nero's order."

Mary pursed her lips. Eyes narrowed, she peered at Mark.

"It was long ago but I have not forgotten the story of what
happened. Peter and his comrades snoring in Gethsemane instead
of keeping watch with my son as he prayed. And later Peter denied
three times that he was a follower. Myself, I would have cursed
Peter for his dereliction and rejection."

"But the Master did not."

"My son had a weakness in that way."

"You cannot believe this!"

Mary leaned back. "There are things that are mine to believe."

"I tell you truly," Mark retorted, "that Peter himself spoke of
the shame of that night. He also told me how the Master forgave
him later, by the Galilean Sea."

"So you say."

Barnabas could contain himself no longer at the end of the
table.

"Peter was a tremendous witness. In Antioch he brought
many to faith in the Master. There and in Rome, in other cities as
well, I have heard his witness. He spoke with passion in a fisher-
man's rough tongue. Many people flocked to hear him."

Mary nodded. "They were all direct in their discourse. Coun-
try folk. The sons of Zebedee, Mary of Magdala, the others. No
hidden meanings to puzzle out. But now he's gone."

"Yes," nodded Mark. "By Emperor's order after the fire that
killed so many of The Community in Rome."

Mary snorted. "Ephesus is still groaning and paying the taxes
that Nero levied to construct new quarters for the Senators and
other men of wealth on the ruins of the old."

"And the death of Paul? You have heard of that also?"

"Yes. No crucifixion for him, they tell me. A Roman citizen
rather than a Galilean bumpkin." Mary gave a sarcastic laugh.
"Killed decently by hanging. Rome has strange ways."

She thought for a moment and then continued.

"Paul came to see me when he was in the city below teaching the Way of my son at the School of Tyrannus. Oh, I could tell you a story about him, if that's why you've come. Proud of his learning, Paul was. Studied under Gamaliel in Jerusalem."

"As did I," Barnabas murmured.

Her eyes grew angry. "Jerusalem!"

"Mistress," Mark quietly continued, "Peter and Paul both faithfully followed the Way of your son."

"Does that excuse Peter his denial? Or Paul—his persecution of others in the name of God?"

"Mama!" Elizabeth exclaimed. She turned to Mark and Barnabas. "Please. Those days long ago sometimes are like yesterday to her." To her mother she said, "Calm, Mama. Calm, calm."

"I'm perfectly calm!" Mary snapped.

There was quiet for a moment. Mark took a sip of wine. He spoke quietly.

"I am sorry if we have offended you. Peter and Paul—their story is done."

"Enough! Tell me plainly why you are here."

Mark and Mary stared evenly at each other before the man replied.

"I am writing an account of your son, our Master. It is compiled from many sources and is near completion. Most of it concerns the last week in Jerusalem."

Mary nodded. "The week that began with high hopes and eager expectations but ended in horror."

"And then joy on the morning after Sabbath," added Barnabas.

"So some say." Mary glanced at Mark. "Is your account a glorification of him, as the pagans do?"

Mark was silent as Barnabas responded, speaking bluntly. "No, not as the pagans do. It is not the history of an Alexander or an Augustus. It is the true tale of the Son of Man, who died a cruel death as the rejected Messiah. The Master was destined for death. He knew his teaching of a new Way, the Way of God the Father, would bring a confrontation with religious and political leaders who wanted no challenge to their power and status."

"Enough!" Mark told his cousin firmly. He turned to Mary. "Please, I need your help."

"My help! You who have traveled with Paul and listened to Peter? What help can a tired old woman give you?"

For a moment, Mark's eyes watched her face filled with anger.

"It was a very difficult time for you," he said softly. "To lose a son in such a way."

"I do not wish to speak of it," retorted Mary. "Events long ago and far away. I have found peace here."

"Forgive us, Mary. I wish to speak to you of earlier times."

Mary erupted, her speech hurried. "The brutal mockery of it all! Innocent of charges against him! Executed between two thieves instead of Barabbas, that murderous criminal. Over his head a pine board that proclaimed him King of the Jews. A warning to other upstarts that this cruelty is what awaited them also."

Her eyes flashed. "And what have you?" Her head turned from one man to the other. "Do you have sons who are willing to die for him as my James did?"

"Calm, Mama, please!" Elizabeth cried.

There was a tense silence, broken at last by Barnabas.

"Peter and Paul were willing. I pray that Mark and I also will be willing if we are put to the test."

Mark raised a hand to silence him. He addressed Mary.

"Please. We are not here to speak of Jerusalem long ago. Please. We need your help with much earlier years."

His voice was calm and soothing. The tension evident in Mary's face subsided.

"I will state again why we are here. Your son learned so much from Joseph and you. His knowledge of scripture began in his childhood. That is why we have come, to hear stories of his growth to manhood before he went to his kinsman, John the baptizer."

Mary sighed. "Ah, the old stories. Others have come to question me. I kept my silence."

"Before Peter's death." Mark went on, "we heard so many stories from him. And other events were told to us when we recently visited Galilee."

Barnabas spoke. "From Paul we learned what he had heard of the Master's teachings. Paul was very clear with us that stories of the childhood of Jesus might be helpful among the Gentiles."

Mary replied with a voice filled with sarcasm.

"Oh, yes. Let us bring more Gentiles in. A whole world of Gentiles! You can tell them this from Mary, his mother. My firstborn was always exceptional. Every day was filled with blissful peace and joy. Of course, there were six other children along the way, accounts to keep for a busy husband with an expanding trade, wash to get done, meals to prepare, animals to be fed as well, the cow milked, and the stalls cleaned." She snorted again. "Holy Mother, indeed."

She held her gnarled hands up and turned them from front to back. "What tales do these hands relate, hmm?"

Mark glanced from Barnabas to Mary. "Please, you two." He nodded to Elizabeth. "Your daughter is right. Calm yourselves. Let us breathe normally."

He laid his hands palm down on the table.

"I will begin again. I have a commission from Peter."

"Peter is dead, as is Paul."

Mark smiled. "Perhaps we call it that but I believe they live among the blessed now."

"As does Joseph, my husband. A righteous man."

Mark nodded. "Please, hear me out."

Mary leaned back as Mark continued.

"Peter and I had long conversations in Rome in the weeks before he, like your son, was crucified. There are revolts brewing all around the Empire for reasons more than the taxes Nero has levied to rebuild inner Rome after the fire. Peter believed a double test of faith is upon us. One is that believers are falling away among those who believed the Master would return quickly. He has not. Among the Thessalonians, the Cappadocians, even in Antioch and Alexandria, skeptics have arisen who are bold to say the Way is based on falsehood. The ambitious striving and self-assurance of such men seems to answer the doubts of a significant number of the former faithful. Their new masters of faith attract them to ways contrary to the true Way.

"The other test arises from places of renewed rebellion within the Empire. In Judea, Galilee and elsewhere, false messiahs have sprung up, calling anew for the overthrow of Roman rule. Such men scoff at the Way of the Master. Many of those who formerly were faithful are now joining the militants, whose lives are bent on destruction and ruin rather than on patient endurance in affliction."

"Yes," Elizabeth spoke up. "I have heard such talk in The Community in Ephesus from those who question the Elders."

Her mother eyed Mark. "And the commission you have been given?"

Mark leaned closer.

"I composing an account. Barnabas is my scribe. But almost nothing is known of the Master's life before his baptism, an old ritual given new meaning in turbulent times. All the events that Peter and the others experienced occurred after Jesus called them to follow him. We have many details from Galilee and Judea of those events, but I need your help with the earlier days."

"It will not be a glorification, then?"

"No. It will be the beginning of my account. The coming of the Good News. I mean it to inspire those who are new in faith and to support those who believed from the beginning."

"An account of my son's life and death."

Mark gave her a long look before continuing.

"An account of his life and death and life again." He turned his hands on the table palms up. "It has been more than thirty years. Many of the faithful believed he would return in triumph by now, leading all the angels of heaven to form the Kingdom of God on earth."

Barnabas nodded and spoke. "Peter said a clear account of what happened is needed in these troubled times. It will remind the weak and fainthearted that we may trust the Master and know him truly as the Son of the Most High."

"*My* son," said Mary.

"Yes, fully human," agreed Mark. "But one sent from God to free us from the barriers that separate us from one another. He helps us to see all people with the eyes of God."

Mary pursed her lips. "Quite an undertaking, this account of yours."

"It is almost finished. I wish to keep it brief enough so that it may be read out at The Community meetings, here in Ephesus and elsewhere. To be read wholly, or in successive parts before the Meal of Remembrance." His eyes were serious. "I need your help with the beginning."

He paused before continuing. "But first there is one matter in which your clarification is essential. You have spoken of your husband. Joseph."

"A holy man. A good husband. A devoted father."

Barnabas spoke. "There are some who say—" He paused and glanced at Mark. Mark nodded.

Barnabas continued. "There are some who say Joseph was not the father of Jesus. Some other man. Perhaps a Roman soldier."

"Rubbish," Mary muttered.

"We must be truthful, you see." Mark said.

Barnabas nodded and spoke emphatically. "One example. We have been told that your betrothal to Joseph extended far longer than usual. The reason? Allegedly a long visit to your kinswoman in Jerusalem. When you returned your womb was large with child. The child of a man of Cana or of someone whom you met in Jerusalem."

Mary slapped both hands on the table and scowled. "Rubbish!" she repeated.

"I will speak plainly," Mark calmly continued. "We do not fear what is true. What matters is the open tomb on the day after Sabbath. The beginning for us is the inner meaning of your son's baptism by John. Perhaps he was a bastard son, adopted at the Jordan River to be the Son of the Most High."

"No!" hissed Mary. "That is falsehood!"

No one spoke.

"Mama?" Elizabeth reached for her mother's hand but Mary moved it away. She raised her head and glared at Mark and Barnabas.

"Such lies! Very well, I will tell you the true story."

Mark smiled. "Thank you."

"But not today. Today there has been too much excitement. I must rest."

Mark frowned. "But we have barely begun."

"I need to think the old matters through. To be able to speak of them in an orderly way for the account that you propose to write."

"Of course," Mark nodded. "We did not wish to burden you so. But the truth of these matters is important."

"I agree."

The two men rose. "We will begin in late morning tomorrow if that is all right."

"Yes." Mary did not return Mark's smile. She was remembering those days so long ago. "Tomorrow."

THREE

MARY USUALLY SLEPT SOUNDLY but that night she drifted in and out of a light slumber, stirred by the conversation of the day.

The visit of the two men brought back a vivid memory of the last day in Jerusalem and the sights and sounds and smells that were etched in her remembering. The hill. The three crosses. The foul odor of blood, human excrement, and piss. The food vendors and the wine sellers, hawking their wares amidst the crowd. And that one man, that odious man who stank from his sweat on the warm day. He approached the disciple John and her, smirking as he shook three wineskins turned shekel collectors. The coins jingled loudly. He pushed her aside and spoke to John.

"And how about you, my good man. Only a shekel to choose the time of death of the one in the middle, poor bastard. Three choices. Only a shekel!" He shook the wineskins vigorously.

"Get away before I knee you in your privates!" John retorted.

The man backed away. "Oh, there's plenty who'll pay. And one will be a rich man! Pity you won't." He laughed as he turned to continue working the crowd.

John put his arm around her and held her close as she shuddered. She was at an angle to the men mounted on horses, surveying the crowd. One, younger than the rest, met her glance with an unsmiling appraisal. He wore the garments of the Chief Priest's household. She averted her eyes, but when she glanced his way again, he was still watching her.

She awoke and turned on her side.

"A dream. Only a dream," she murmured to herself. "Long ago. Over and done."

She dozed. Her restless limbs quieted. She fell into a deeper sleep and dreamed again.

She was standing at the side of the large dry-stone pen constructed by Lazarus and his nephew Amos many years ago. The low circular pen was on a level place carved out of the hillside below the farmhouse in which Lazarus, Amos and Rebecca had lived. There was a lovely view down the pathway that led to the city, the metropolis of Ephesus, almost as populous as Rome.

The pen was home in the summer to two workhorses of Amos that pulled to the cottage the trees hewn in the forest. There they were cut and trimmed for sale as lumber.

No workhorses were present, only a white stallion at the far side of the pen. He was turned away from her. She could hear the sighing of the wind in the treetops.

As she walked closer to the pen, she felt a warm breeze caress her face.

The horse flicked the summer flies away with his tail, oblivious to her presence until she called to him. Then his head turned toward her. They regarded one another, horse and human, both with an even unblinking gaze. Neither moved.

At last the large head turned away. She was tempted to walk around the pen to come closer to the stallion, but a sudden feeling of peace filled her and she remained still.

She slept soundly through the remainder of the night.

When she awoke, dawn was breaking. The details of the dream remained clear.

Amos came to the cottage later. He brought fresh fruit and cheese that Rebecca had churned from their cow's milk and let ripen in the spring.

Mary asked him if he had a new horse to help with his farm work. A white stallion.

He smiled. "Not enough Roman coins in hand for another horse. Why do you ask?"

"A dream I had in the night. A white stallion was in your pen."

Amos laughed. "Next time ask him to hang around. I could use another horse now that I'm felling trees further back in the woods."

Four

THE MORNING WAS SUNNY. Again they sat at the table in the small house while Elizabeth took her turn in the garden, watched over by Felix.

"I hope you slept well?" inquired Mark.

"Well enough." Mary replied curtly. "I am calmer now."

"I will not press the matter about Joseph today."

"I wish for the truth to be told."

"In due time. Here is how we plan to proceed. I will ask a series of questions about your son's early days. Barnabas has a slate and a stylus. He will make brief notes to remind us of the conversation."

Mary was silent, gazing down at the table. At last she spoke.

"No. Not that way. Let *me* tell *you* the beginning. It will answer some of your questions. If you wish to proceed differently, you may use the idle tales of others. I am sure there are old crones still alive in Nazareth who can spin entertaining tales of the young Jesus, the magician, the miracle worker. But take care. I have even heard rumors that for a few shekels you can be shown my burial site in Nazareth or elsewhere." She pursed her lips. "But as you can see, I am not in my grave yet."

Mark folded his hands on the table. "Very well. But please answer one of my questions first. Why are you called the Rabbi's daughter? Barnabas and I, in all our travels, had never heard that name until we reached Ephesus."

"It is just as well."

"Are you a Rabbi's daughter?"

"Yes, a good man. Quite advanced for the times. He believed that girls should receive schooling as well as the boys."

"I see. That was in Nazareth?"

"No. In Cana."

"I see. But why are you called by that name in Ephesus?"

Mary sighed. "It was because of fear years ago. I see no need for it now, but the name persists. The name was given me in the terrible days when everyone feared that others would be the next to die. I was his mother. Kill the seedling, kill the source."

"Are you still fearful?"

She gave a short laugh. "I am old now and most days I would welcome death as a friend. But the Elders in The Community insist I continue to use the name in Ephesus lest attention be drawn to those in the house gatherings after the Sabbath day. 'The Master and his Way are the proper focus,' they have said to me many times."

"I have been told that you no longer attend the house gatherings."

"No. With more and more Greeks in the city joining The Community I am not comfortable with the new prayers, the hymns, and the exhortations. Until a few years ago I did attend Sabbath services at the synagogue."

"How were they?"

"A comfort. The old traditions and festival observances." She looked at him. "You may have heard that there are growing tensions about Jews who follow the Way worshiping in the synagogue on the Sabbath."

"Yes. It is also a tension in Antioch and, I have heard, in Alexandria as well."

Mark shifted on the bench on his side of the table.

"How did a Rabbi's daughter in Cana end up in Nazareth?"

Mary smiled. "The usual way. Arrangements were made and I was betrothed to a quite prosperous man in Nazareth. He was well versed in scripture and so found favor with my father."

"The man was Joseph?"

"Yes."

"Was he training to be a rabbi?"

Mary smiled. "No. He had a large and profitable carpentry trade. He also had a close friend who was a stonemason. Joseph supplied him with the crossbeams, doors and shutters in building new homes in Nazareth and the surrounding area."

She glanced down the table at Barnabas. "I hear you scribbling."

"Now, now," soothed Mark. "A few notes only."

She leaned back. "When Paul visited he told me there was a struggle going on in Ephesus between members of The Community and the larger population who worshiped the goddess Artemis at her Temple. He was lucky to escape with his life."

Mark grimaced. "Barnabas has told me of that. He was with Paul then. Paul was about to debate the chief priest of the goddess in the amphitheater when the crowd became unruly and his disciples pulled him away." He glanced at Barnabas. "He and others went on to Macedonia."

Mary looked down at the table.

"He told me that I was in danger of becoming a goddess for the Greeks who worship with The Community. An alternative to Artemis."

There was a sudden silence. Mark's gaze was steady. Barnabas stopped scribbling.

"Is that why you wish nothing to be said about you?" asked Mark.

"It was not my doing. I am the mother of Jesus. But only a few members of The Community knew me as that. Several of the Greek silversmiths knew. Paul told the Elders that I should continue to be referred to only as 'the Rabbi's daughter.'"

Mark frowned. "And the Rabbi here in Ephesus—does he have a daughter?"

"No. He was blessed with five sons. The Rabbi before him— his wife bore him twin boys."

"And you? We have met your daughter, Elizabeth." Mark nodded at her. "And Rebecca in the farmhouse down the hill. Others?"

Mary sighed and counted out the names on her fingers. "Five others. Jesus, James, Little Joseph, Judah, and Simon."

"Where are the last three now?"

Mary stiffened.

"Why do you ask? So that you may hound them?"

"No." Mark sighed. "I understand. Here I am, a stranger, soliciting information that you fear may be altered or used against you and your family." He put his hands palms down on the table.

"You have not let me tell my story the way I wish. I think you should go now," murmured Mary.

"No!" Barnabas exclaimed from the end of the table. "Call your daughter. She may help."

"Very well."

Mary rose from the table and went to the door.

"Elizabeth, come here, please."

When Elizabeth entered the room, Barnabas stood.

"Forgive my frankness but we need to reassure your mother that we are not enemies. In years past were you at gatherings of The Community?"

"Mama?"

"Answer him, my dear."

"Yes."

"During the years when Paul visited?"

"The second time. The time that concluded when Demetrius the head of the silversmith guild caused an uproar in the amphitheater."

"I was one of those with Paul. Do you recall me?"

She gazed at him for a moment.

"Yes." She blushed and turned to her mother with a rush of words.

"Mama, you remember. You were staying home those days, and when I returned from the city you asked me for news and I told you about the man, one of Paul's disciples, who bore a remarkable resemblance to brother James. I was quite startled when I saw him at the Remembrance Meal."

"And this is the man."

"Yes."

Barnabas turned to Mary. "I am the man. Mark is not only my cousin, he also is my brother in the Lord. We are here in friendship and ask your help in Mark's account."

"Thank you, daughter," Mary drily said. "Back to your gardening now. I hope you are not distracting Felix from his duties."

Elizabeth blushed again. "No, Mama. He tells me news of Ephesus but is careful to keep his eyes on the woods around us and the pathway down the hill."

She curtsied and left. Mary gestured to Barnabas. "Please, sit." They both sat.

"Little Joseph has a carpentry shop in Tiberias. Judah manages sheep for an estate owner near Caesarea Maritime, and Simon also has a carpentry shop—in Damascus. He is an Elder in the Damascus Community."

"None of them are troubled by the authorities?"

"They were hidden by friends in the early years."

"But no longer."

"They did not attract crowds as my oldest had done. As it was feared that I would. As James later did also. The authorities may have deemed the others harmless and lost interest."

"And you?"

Mary gave a snort. "I have heard reports of three places where I am buried. But you see me. I am an old woman tending her garden in the hills above Ephesus. There are far more important distractions now, if what you tell me about Peter's foreboding is accurate."

"May I speak to Little Joseph, Judah, and Simon?"

Her mouth tightened. "You will do as you wish but I prefer not."

"I will make you a bargain. Tell me more about the Master's childhood as he grew to manhood." He held his hands up, palms almost touching. "Just this much, and I will not trouble the others."

"I have your promise?"

"Yes," agreed Mark. "Now tell us the beginning."

Mary clasped her hands and looked sternly at each man in turn.

"I want you to understand that what I now tell you my son did not know until after his father's death."

"So, Joseph indeed was his father?" It was a question from Mark. He and Barnabas exchanged glances.

"He was an excellent father."

"We have wondered."

"Oh, the beginning. That was different, as I will tell you. But until this day I have told only my son what I now tell you." She paused. "That's not quite true. My parents knew because of the circumstances. And his parents. Joseph's. And my kinswoman, Elizabeth, mother of John the baptizer. I assisted in his birth."

She paused for a moment. "I was not evident with child yet when I went to her. When I returned, the baby was a toddler. There had been no wedding in Cana. That may be why the rumors began about another man, a Roman soldier, or someone else."

"Ah," breathed Mark.

"Yes. Joseph and I never spoke about the actual circumstances, nor did the few others who knew. Years later, on his deathbed, Joseph made me promise that I at last would tell our son. But the days and weeks that followed were busy ones. I said nothing. Then one day our kinsman John came to visit. He had been with one of the Essene communities and in a vision saw Jesus and himself at the river Jordan. He came to us to claim Jesus as his first disciple."

"And your son went?" Barnabas asked.

"No. He declined. He honored John's vision but thought it to have a different meaning. John went away in a huff and found other disciples. However, because of his visit I began to tell Jesus what I now tell you. And after hearing it, he did finally go to John, but not to stay. He went into the Judean Desert for a time of fasting and prayer. When he returned he was emaciated, but, oh, how his eyes glowed with conviction and purpose!"

She gave a wistful smile to the two listeners.

"I have long thought that if only I had kept silent, he would have remained in Nazareth. It was as though my telling brought his awakening to what he was to do." She sighed. "But I promised his father that I would tell him. So I did. And now I tell you."

FIVE

"MY FATHER, SERAIAH, WAS Rabbi of the synagogue in Cana. He was devoted to his study of the Law and the Prophets and did not marry my mother until later in life. She was older, past the usual age of marriage. I was born soon after, their only child. My father also was an only child. They hoped for more children but it was not to be. Of Mother's family, only a younger brother remained. Cleopas. Mother's parents were both gone but her father left Mother money for herself and Cleopas. Uncle Cleopas was a great support, but when I was a young child he moved from Cana to Nazareth and took a wife. Mother helped with the bride-price he needed for his wife."

Mark interrupted her. "What does this have to do with your son?"

"It is a tightly woven story. Have patience."

She continued. "As a girl I learned not only the care of a home but also more worldly things. My father was quite progressive for his times. He held religious school for the boys, as rabbis do. He also formed one for the girls, twelve of us, and gave us nicknames from the Twelve Tribes. We learned about the Law and the Prophets as well as stories from our history. The Patriarchs. Moses and Joshua and the others. Mighty King David. The later destruction of the Temple in Jerusalem and the rebuilding. The great captivity in Babylon. The revolts that arose and failed.

"We also were taught Greek. What a strange language compared to ours! But Father said it was important for us as future wives to know how to converse with the Greek traders in the marketplace."

"How did you meet Joseph?"

"Through Uncle Cleopas. Joseph's father began a carpentry shop in Nazareth but had grown to an age when he had difficulty with the tools. Mostly he sat in the garden and dozed. Cleopas told my parents that Joseph had taken over the shop and seemed quite an up-and-comer who had recently expanded into construction with a friend who was a stonemason.

"In my fifteenth year, I overheard a conversation between my parents. They were discussing a suitable match—this Joseph of Nazareth. Twice as old as I he was, but well settled and financially prepared for marriage. Although he was not a rabbi, he was considered quite knowledgeable in religious matters. My father had spoken to his father and there was a tentative agreement between them. Mother insisted that I meet Joseph and give my consent. Father grumbled and sputtered, but in the end she had her way."

She fell silent, remembering.

"And you met him," prodded Barnabas.

"Oh yes." She smiled at the memory. "I must have seemed terribly prim and shy, but goodness, he was twice as old as I, which made him seem ancient, and he was such a bear of a man, though well spoken!"

"The betrothal agreement was made?"

"Not at first sight! My parents were eavesdropping behind the doorway curtain. Suddenly Mother came bustling through and firmly suggested that we should take a walk though the village so that I might tell him of my homemaking skills."

"So much for not holding to old customs," Mark murmured.

Mary turned to him and smiled broadly. "Though she approved of Father's class for young women, she feared that too much mention of my intellectual pursuits would put a damper on the betrothal.

"So he and I took our walk up one street of Cana and down another. I was careful to listen to his plans for expanding his work. I smiled and nodded most agreeably and mentioned nothing about the Law and the Prophets or history or Greek traders. And by the end of our walk I thought him to be a good and thoughtful man, so the plans for our betrothal were all right."

"A very pleasant tale," remarked Barnabas.

"The difficult part of my story came later."

A long silence. The two men waited. At last she cleared her throat and continued.

"The betrothal was announced in both Cana and Nazareth. The day afterwards my parents escorted me to the groom's house, as was the custom. There we met Joseph's elderly parents. It was a preliminary meeting. Once the details were settled by the two fathers I would be spending a great deal of time at their house. After the wedding feast, it would be our home as well as the home of Joseph's parents.

"We met with Joseph's parents. They were thrilled that their son was to marry a rabbi's daughter, and my mother spoke quite positively about the treasure of household skills I would bring to their home. At the end of our conversation the two fathers were to settle on the bride-price and date for the marriage. Mother and I left them chatting and returned home.

"It was a warm spring evening. Father returned, delighted about the arrangements that had been made. After the supper dishes were washed, I knew he and Mother wanted to talk, so I told Mother that I was going to sit in the garden for a bit of fresh air. Our garden was a lovely, peaceful place, well suited to collecting my thoughts. We had a small fountain near the street and beautiful blooming flowers all around, with rows of vegetables on the inward side stretching to the far end of the garden.

"I sat on a bench near the gate and wondered what life with Joseph would bring. I knew that my parents loved me. We were very close. How would life be once I was living in Nazareth, separated from everything that home meant to me? My mother's easy humor and common sense, my father's wisdom and instruction about the wider world, and, most of all, the wonderful stories I loved to hear about their own parents and grandparents. Some times I would sit for hours just listening to such family stories. I never tired of them.

"Those days soon would end. What was to come in my marriage to Joseph? Would he be kind and caring, willing to patiently explain things to his young wife? Or would he be one of those men who are aloof and distant and harsh? And what about our children—what kind of father would he be?

"But that was all in the future for me as a girl in her fifteenth year. The point is—I was immersed in my thoughts, and even feeling a little sorry for myself.

"And now to what happened in that garden long ago."

Mary paused to take a deep breath. She searched Mark's face and then her gaze dropped as she continued.

"I was startled by a soft voice calling to me, 'Mary.'

"A man dressed in a white cloak was standing on the garden path next to me. His face and his cloak shone with a light that kept moving slightly, wavering in the late afternoon sunlight."

"Shimmering?" Mark asked.

"Yes. He smiled at me as I looked up at him. He said, 'Do not be afraid. I am Gabriel, messenger of the Lord.'"

Mark and Barnabas exchanged glances.

"The messenger in the Book of Daniel," Barnabas whispered. He began to write on his slate.

Mary nodded. "Yes, as I learned later."

"You speak so calmly," said Mark. "Weren't you frightened?"

"No. As I looked at him, his face and cloak wavered, brighter and then dimmer. But I was not afraid. There was such a great sense of calm and peace about him."

Mark leaned toward her. "Was it a vision you were having?"

"No. The garden was quite real. The scent of the flowers was heavy in the air, and the bees were buzzing about. And the man standing by me had the loveliest, tender smile as he looked at me."

"What then?"

"He told me—" She took a deep breath. "He told me that I was chosen by the Lord to bear a special child but nothing would happen without my assent. And then he waited. I replied, 'I must tell Joseph this good news!' He was silent.

"'Joseph will be the father?' I asked him. It all sounded strange to me, coming immediately after my thoughts of what the future might hold.

"'No,' he replied.

"I said something like, 'Thank you for this offer but I am betrothed to Joseph and am a virgin.'

"My visitor smiled. 'Joseph indeed will be your husband and be a good father to your son and to the other children you will bear. But that is in your future.'

"My breath was taken away by what I was hearing. The man's eyes turned serious and he said, 'Mary, you are needed for this task by the Lord. It is a new beginning. It will not take place without *you*.'"

Mark let out his own breath. "A new beginning. Please think carefully. Those words exactly?"

"It is a new beginning," Mary replied.

"And you said yes."

"I did. Yes."

"And then?"

"Then Gabriel smiled with a joyous smile and he reached out both hands and placed them on my head. He spoke in a tongue I did not know and still do not, though I have heard many languages since I came to Ephesus. As he spoke I felt warmth within my midsection that grew and grew until I felt as though my whole body was glowing. He then spoke in our own tongue, wonderful words I scarcely can remember, a long praise hymn to the Lord, honoring me for all that would come about through this child I was to bear. It ended and he told me that the child was to be named Jesus. And he told me of things to come."

Mary's gaze dropped. "He said nothing of Jerusalem or the horror of the hill outside the city."

She sighed and was quiet.

"Please," Mark urged. "What then?"

"He finished and the warmth receded and I felt a sudden listlessness as though I were about to faint. I did not, but when I lifted my gaze he was gone."

Barnabas peered at her. "This is not some childhood dream? It truly happened?"

"Yes. As I have said."

"You are telling us that Joseph was not the father of Jesus?"

"Yes," replied Mary.

Mark peered at her keenly. "You were a young maiden. You did not know how such things happen. But now, looking back, did the visitor, this Gabriel, penetrate you in any way?"

A great stillness settled on the room. At last Mary spoke in a calm voice.

"Maidens are not ignorant of such matters. Truly, he laid his hands upon my head. That is all."

She smiled. "When I tell you now, it sounds like one of the Greek stories we would laugh at in my father's class. Zeus and the gods and what that lot would do. And Olympias, mother of Alexander the Great, claiming her son was the result of a lightning flash to her womb. Pagan stories! Do you wish such a thing in your account, Mark?"

"I seek the truth of what happened."

Mary glanced at the two men and sighed. "I am tired with the remembering. It may be best for us to continue at a later time."

Mark rose, "Your throat must be dry. Perhaps a cup of water will help." He went to the open kitchen nearby, glancing at Barnabas as he went. "Barnabas?"

"Not for me."

Mark returned to the table with a cup of water. He set it before Mary.

"Please, we want to hear the rest," he said.

She drank the cupful. "Very well. This is the hard part."

Six

"It was my secret," Mary continued. "I told no one. Mother was giving me instruction daily on how I was to do things in my new life. Days passed and I began to think it truly had been a beautiful daydream brought on by my fears of going to a strange new house. But then . . . "

She broke off and looked from Mark to Barnabas and back again.

"You are grown men. Surely you must know about the rites women observe when they have their monthly blood. The special arrangements."

They nodded.

"It was fairly new to me, but I for a short while had always been regular in my time of the month. The time passed. With a sinking feeling I counted carefully the days I was past due. I waited for another week. Nothing. My mother had noticed, and one afternoon she spoke to me directly about it. I did not know what to say—I was so young then. Question after question. I finally told her what I have told you just now."

"And?"

"She searched my face for a moment and then she laughed and told me I was a silly thing and I needed to eat more. She said she knew positively that I had not been with any man and what I said was impossible.

"This state of affairs went on for another week of no bleeding, at the end of which she took me to my father's study and had me repeat what I had said to her.

"Father looked at me sternly. 'Tell me truly, have you been with a man in the way to make a child?'

"I said 'no.' He looked at my mother. He asked her if there was any possibility I had been with a man. Mother said 'no' and she began to weep.

"'How can this be true,' she cried. 'We have always been faithful to the Lord. Why has this happened to upright people? Our child, our only child, whom we love! We must do something, but what?'

"My father told her to calm herself and said they needed to think things through."

Mary paused, remembering. "And then?" Mark prompted her.

"Long faces around the house. He and my mother talked for quite a while, but the door to his study was closed firmly and I could hear nothing. The next day my father arranged a meeting with Joseph and his parents. Such an honorable man, my father!

"But Joseph was busy with matters in the shop. So it was several days before we met with them. And every morning before we went to Nazareth Mother asked me if there was any change. There was no change. So off we three went to Nazareth at last.

"Joseph was finishing up a carpentry project. He had asked his parents to greet us and he would be along shortly. We were ushered into the dining room and took our seats around the table. After a few pleasantries, a long silence followed.

"My father, so honor bound to do the right thing, broke the silence by asking if Joseph would be along soon. Joseph's mother said it was quite agreeable to him for us to go ahead and speak of whatever we wished to see them about."

Mary sighed. "So. After a few minutes of waiting, Father asked me to give my account once more in front of Joseph's parents. I was frightened, but I did. Throughout my brief recital, Joseph's father nodded pleasantly at me but the face of Joseph's mother grew harder and harder. When I finished, there was a long cold silence.

"At last, Joseph's father cleared his throat several times and said, 'Well.'

"Father had kept his eyes on him throughout my account and now said, 'My wife and I believe our daughter. I realize it is a difficult tale to comprehend. I ask you to do so.'

"Silence. Father and Mother joined hands. At last, Father nodded and spoke softly.

"'It may be too difficult for you. You are entitled to break the betrothal covenant if you wish.'

"Joseph's father beamed at me and said, 'She certainly is a lovely child. Imagine! A messenger from the Lord!'

"Joseph's mother gave a loud sniff and leaned forward. She studied me and then said. 'A young, pretty face goes best with such a pious story. But I want my son to know of the matter before any more is said. I will go fetch him from his work and tell him of your sorry tale before we return.'

"She rose and left the room.

"It was perfectly clear to everyone but Joseph's father what was about to happen. The betrothal would end. My family would be disgraced forever and probably have to move to another town. I would be tainted goods and never marry.

"The wait seemed to go on forever.

"From somewhere on the other side of the house, we heard voices, muffled by the distance, the mother's voice angry and high pitched. Occasionally it was interrupted by Joseph's lower tone. The voices stopped and there were footsteps. Joseph's mother swished through the doorway curtain. She sat with a thump in her chair and crossed her arms over her chest.

"'He is thinking of what to say.' She smiled at me, a wintry smile.

"More waiting. The air grew heavy in the room. I began to feel quite faint. My mother started to weep.

"At last the doorway curtain was pushed aside and Joseph entered. He looked only at me with a direct gaze. I returned it without flinching. At last he spoke. I have never forgotten his words.

"'Mary, this account that my mother reports to me is a strange one indeed. You are young and as yet not acquainted with the ways of the world.'

"He paused. Our eyes remained locked. I kept silent.

"'Do you swear by the Lord that you have spoken truly?'

"'Yes.'

"'You swear by the Lord that you have been with no man?'

"'I do. No man.'

"He glanced at his parents. His father smiled genially at me. His mother spoke, hissing the words like sharp knives. 'An inspection will show the truth of this sorry tale.'

"Joseph raised a hand to silence her. She gave a snort of disapproval and settled in her chair.

"Joseph looked again at me. 'When my mother told me just now of your words, anger rose up in me at your treachery. I could not bear to face you again, such was my rage.'

"He paused and then went on. 'But I told my mother I would come here to see your parents and you face to face. As I crossed to this room, my anger cooled. You are young. I do not wish your life to be ruined. I thought the answer is to end the betrothal quietly and we go our separate ways in Nazareth and Cana. Such things are rare but not unheard of.'

"Joseph looked at me and his eyes softened. 'But you have sworn by the Lord. You are a rabbi's daughter and you know what that means.' He ran a hand through his hair.

"'I cannot believe the Lord acts in the way you describe.'

"Another snort came from his mother.

"'Yet you have told my parents and now me that the Lord has done just that.'

"He paused and there was a mutter from his mother. He raised his eyebrows as he looked at her. When she said nothing more, his gaze returned to me.

"'Yes,' I affirmed.

"His gaze turned harder, more intense. The room was very still except for my mother's steady weeping. Joseph spoke at last.

"'I cannot comprehend what has happened. It is a test of faith.'

"'Yes,' I replied.

"Neither of us blinked in the silence between us.

"'It seems I must trust you,' he said at last.

The Rabbi's Daughter

"His eyes were on mine for another long moment. At last he nodded. 'Very well.'

"He looked at his parents and mine. 'I do not wish the betrothal covenant to be broken. I will honor it and pay the bride-price myself.'

"Mother's weeping ended with a choked sob. She reached over and took my hand. Father let out a long sigh of withheld breath.

"Scowling, Joseph's mother hugged herself more tightly. Her son said to her, 'There will be no gossip, Mother. Not a word outside this house. This is my command. Do you understand?'

"She muttered, 'As you wish, my son.'

"Joseph's father gave me a huge smile and slapped his hands on the table. 'Good!' he said. 'Now that that's settled, I'm off to the garden again.' He stood. 'Imagine! A messenger from the Lord!'"

Mary's voice ceased. She realized with a start that her hand had been tightly holding the hand of Mark for some time. Embarrassed, she released his hand and looked about. The stylus scratching on the slate ceased.

"That was how his life came to be. My son Jesus." She began to weep. "And it ended in excruciating pain on a hill outside Jerusalem."

Elizabeth appeared in the doorway.

"Mama! Are you all right?" Angrily she shook her fist at Mark and Barnabas.

"What have you stirred up? She is not that strong, you know!"

"It is something she wanted to tell us," Mark quietly replied. "Something very important. But the telling of it tired her." He nodded at Elizabeth. "You are a loving daughter. We will return tomorrow and learn whether we are welcome or not."

The two men stood and said their farewells to Mary, who remained hunched over the table.

Elizabeth turned in the doorway and watched them gesture to Felix. She walked out to him as he was crossing the yard and he paused briefly to speak to her. Then Felix joined the two men and the three of them walked down the hill. Mark and Barnabas were engaged in serious conversation.

Elizabeth hurried back to her mother, who was still seated at the table.

"Mother, I must tell you something."

"Yes?" Mary dried her tears.

"This visit is not completely a surprise, and I will tell you why. Felix is not unknown to me. He is employed as the head of the guardsmen for the Chief Elder in Ephesus."

Mary smiled wanly. "He seems like a good person. Is he a member of The Community?"

"Oh, yes. And there are times after the Meal of Remembrance that we have spoken." Elizabeth hastened on. "Recently he told me of the arrival of two men in Ephesus. Men who spoke to the Chief Elder about an interview with you." She blushed. "Felix is not married."

"Oh. You are close."

Elizabeth nodded. "Yes." She added, "I do not know if something will come of it."

"If it should, you would have my blessing."

"Thank you, Mother. But that is not what I wished to tell you. Felix and I have had conversations during his surveillance here. Just now he said something very strange to me."

"Yes?"

"He was looking at them and he said, 'I have overheard some of their conversations in the evening.'"

"And?"

"'Mark and Barnabas have other purposes here than what they say. Warn your mother to be careful in what she tells them.'"

Mary pushed back from the table and stood.

"They say they want the truth. I will tell them what I know. If it does not fit the story they wish to weave, they are traitors to Jesus my son." She gave a dark look toward Elizabeth. "Your brother."

SEVEN

WHEN SHE RETIRED TO her room for sleep that evening she continued to feel disturbed at what Elizabeth had told her. She sat on the edge of the bed that her husband had made for them so many years before. She unpinned her hair, which she kept up during the day, and began her nightly brushing and combing.

What dark purpose might Mark and Barnabas have? She could think of none. She certainly had quashed the notion of a soldier or someone in Jerusalem being the father of Jesus.

She finished and put brush and comb in the top drawer of a side table.

She knelt by the bed and prayed for guidance in what she would say to the two visitors. And she prayed for a peaceful sleep.

Rising, Mary turned to the oil lamp atop the side table and lowered the flame. Then she crawled onto the bed and pulled the woolen blanket over her.

She slept, a deep, deep sleep into the early hours of the night.

In the final hours of the night, a wind came up and tall trees in the woods outside began to creak as they bent to and fro. The sound roused her to a state of lighter sleep in which she dreamed once more of the white stallion.

Again she was standing at the side of the large circular pen. The stallion was still at the other side of the pen but now he had turned and was facing her. For an immeasurable length of time they stood like that, gazing at each other. Suddenly the stallion whinnied and moved to the center of the pen. Mary felt she ought to do something but could not think of what it might be. She stood rooted in place by the side of the pen. The stallion's large eyes watched her.

She awoke suddenly. She rose from the bed and went to the kitchen to fetch a cup of water. She was puzzled and tried to find some meaning in the dream but could not.

Eight

Morning. There was dew on the grass today. The vivid dream had faded. Despite a sound sleep for much of the night, Mary felt old and worn and moved slowly.

Again they sat at the table, Mark facing her and Barnabas at the end. Mark hesitated before speaking.

"Holy Mother—"

"No more of that!" she snapped.

"I'm sorry. You seem tired. It may be best to wait another day or so before we continue our conversation."

Mary pursed her lips. "I did not mean to be rude. Please, continue. Soon you may go on your way."

Mark cleared his throat.

"Yesterday you told us of the visitation of Gabriel. He told you, 'It is a new beginning.'

Those were his exact words?"

"As I have said."

Mark leaned back in his chair. "Had your parents noticed any change in your appearance after your experience in the garden?"

"Apparently not. Their concern was my pregnancy, which was not showing as yet."

"When you went to the house of Joseph, was anything said by his parents or by Joseph about a change in your appearance?"

"What is it you are asking?"

Barnabas spoke from the end of the table.

"The afternoon of the person in your garden, you described the messenger's appearance as 'wavering.' We took that to mean a shimmering of some sort."

"Yes. At times his face and cloak were clear and then they wavered."

Barnabas nodded. "Mark is asking whether any of this shimmering was transferred to your garments."

"No. I had my usual appearance. Then and later. Why is it of interest?"

"Something Peter and others have told us about the appearance of the Master. After the tomb."

Barnabas persisted. "When Lazarus came to you, was his appearance altered?"

"No."

Mark resumed his questioning.

"After the visit to Joseph and his parents, did any of what you told them get around? Village gossip in Nazareth or Cana?"

"No, nothing."

"Were you treated differently by the townspeople?"

"No. Just as before—respect for the daughter of the Rabbi. There *was* curiosity about the postponement of the marriage date. But my parents announced that I was going to Jerusalem to help my mother's kinswoman in her pregnancy."

"And then?"

"I stayed on in Jerusalem, as you have heard, helping her through the birth of John and for a time afterward."

"John who later became the baptizer?"

"Yes. Then the Census decreed by Augustus came. Joseph sent word that I was to accompany him to Bethlehem."

"You returned to Cana?"

"No. I was almost due. Joseph travelled south and met me in Jerusalem."

Mary smiled. "When he arrived he became quite concerned. He said I looked like I was about to burst. But I reassured him that I could make it to Bethlehem, only a short distance away."

"And Jesus was born in Bethlehem? That story is true?"

"Yes." Mary sighed. "In a stable beside an inn. Something I do not like to remember."

She turned her gaze from Mark to Barnabas and back.

"Why do you wish to know such things?"

Mark glanced at Barnabas before answering.

"There is an elderly woman in Cana who told us not long ago that you had the face of an angel before your child was born."

Mary snorted. "She must be kin to Methusaleh! No one in Cana saw my belly grow."

Barnabas spoke, "She appeared to be quite old. She said your face shone with a heavenly light."

"Oh, come, come! What some old gossips will say for attention!" Mary laughed. "It is commonplace that women carrying a child may look very different. But what a woman feels like is *not* angelic." She cocked her head. "Are either of you wived?"

"No," they both said.

"I thought not. What other tales have you heard?"

"The same woman claims that you yourself were an unusual birth by your own mother."

"Oh, such tittle-tattle. Was she Greek?"

"And another told us that you were born in a high official's house in Jerusalem."

"I hope that in the account you write, Mark, you may put an end to such falsehoods!"

Mark smiled. "Presumably told to burnish the teller's own sense of self-importance."

Mary sighed. "The reality was far different. The delivery was difficult and long. During my recovery we three remained in Bethlehem. Joseph found a carpentry position and arranged for a friend to manage the shop in Nazareth until we could return."

"Those were difficult times," murmured Mark.

"Indeed. Even worse times followed."

She looked at the two men. "No one has told you that true story?"

"You returned to Nazareth?" queried Barnabas.

"No. We went to Egypt."

"What!" Mark exclaimed. "No, we have not heard of that."

"It was a terrible time that troubles me still."

"Say more."

"Such a long, long time ago. What does it matter now?"

"Tell us."

NINE

MARY SHIFTED HER POSITION on the bench.

"Joseph had a dream that saved our lives, though other lives were lost."

"Tell us," Mark repeated.

"It is terrible, almost as terrible as that day of the horror on the hill outside Jerusalem."

"This is completely new to us. We want to hear what happened."

Mary sighed a deep sigh. "It is not good to speak of old horrors. Joseph always said we must have faith. Sometimes faith is a heavy burden."

The room was silent. Through the open door they heard two birds calling. Mary stared down at the table.

"It was a dream of blood."

"How so?"

Mary looked up. "We remained in Bethlehem for some months after Jesus was born." She grimaced. "His was not an easy birthing, and my healing took time. So we stayed on. Joseph found us inexpensive lodging and sent a message to a friend to keep an eye on Joseph's parents and the house.

"As for Joseph, he found work in Bethlehem. We survived, although they were hard times.

"One day magnificently clothed strangers arrived from the East. They oohed and aahed over the baby and told us we truly were blessed to have a son who was meant for great things. Joseph spoke to them. I was preoccupied with my own female problems.

"After they left, Joseph came to me in high excitement. The visitors had given expensive gifts, far more than even five years' profits from the Nazareth shop.

"'Now you can have the very best care,' he proclaimed. But that night he dreamed a dream that was to change our lives dramatically. A dream of blood."

"Yours?"

"If you mean as a woman, no. It was a dream of other women, mothers crying over the bloody bodies of their young children. Soldiers were walking the streets of Bethlehem, knocking on doors and pulling infants and toddlers out, butchering them."

"Dear Lord in heaven!" exclaimed Mark.

"Yes. Joseph woke me before the first cockcrow and whispered these things in my ear. A horrible dream. I tried to calm him, but at the end of the telling, he rose from the bed and declared, 'We must go. Today. *Now.*'"

"How awful."

"I was only half awake. Jesus was by my side, mewing. I struggled to a sitting position and put him to my breast. 'It is only a dream,' I cried. 'Why must we go?'

"He made no reply. Immediately he began packing our few belongings. In a short while he came to the door of the house with our donkey and loaded Jesus and me onto it along with two sacks of our meager belongings and another of his tools. And so we went. To Egypt, the land where long ago another Joseph rose to sit at the right hand of Pharaoh."

"So sudden," Barnabas murmured.

"Uprooted like that, yes. But for a reason. As we traveled we heard along the way stories of how King Herod the Great had received the men from the East. He had inquired of his palace priests where they might go and they told him, Bethlehem."

Mary smiled a wintry smile. "Mark, you and Barnabas believe terrible times are to come. They often have come in my lifetime."

"Tell us," Mark said quietly. "The soldiers in Joseph's dream—Herod's soldiers?"

"Yes. It was in the last year of Herod's reign. Lost in his fears of conspiracies on all sides. Some said he had gone mad. Many of his own wives and children—poisoned or executed. And those children in Bethlehem—two years of age or younger. He had to root out the threat from a future rival.

"A dream," said Mary. "That's what Joseph had. Through a sign from God we were spared. But not the others. Thirty or more infants and young children torn from their mothers' arms and savagely murdered."

She glanced at Mark and Barnabas. "But not my son. Not Jesus. He was spared for a reason. But those children—they were all special to their mothers, too. I sometimes wonder what the meaning of it is.

"Through the years I came to believe my son truly was special. I never imagined that brutality would claim him also. On a cross outside Jerusalem."

She sighed and stood. "I must rest for a brief time. Elizabeth is bringing food for the midday meal from my daughter's house down the hill. Please eat. If you wish to stay, we will resume afterwards."

"Very well," said Mark. "After the meal, Barnabas and I will take a walk. We hope to find you rested on our return."

Ten

THE CONVERSATION RESUMED AFTER the two men's passage around the garden.

"When did you return from Egypt?" asked Barnabas.

Mary thought. "It was when my son began to walk. I had just realized I was pregnant again."

Mark interrupted. "Joseph was the father?"

"Oh, yes. Joseph definitely was the father; father of James and all the others, too. We both came from a family of only one child. We wanted more. Joseph spoke with me often about his plans to expand the carpentry shop when we returned to Nazareth. He dreamed of having many sons who would help out."

She paused. "Herod was dead. Messages from Galilee told us all was safe enough in the north. During our absence Joseph's father had died also. His mother was growing feeble and wanted a pair of young hands to help her with the household. My parents were eager to visit with their grandchild."

"You were aware that your firstborn was special?" Mark asked.

Mary laughed. "I must be careful with my words, I see. Here you are, two unmarried men. You have no children of your own."

"Spiritual children," protested Barnabas.

"Yes, yes, of course. I have heard that phrase spoken in The Community in Ephesus. All fine and good. But to truly have your own. They all are special, but the firstborn is the most special of all. That was my meaning."

"How was Jesus special?" asked Mark.

"Oh, I could tell you hundreds of stories. But it would be winter before I finished and you need to conclude your account long before then."

"Pick one."

"He was careful and caring with James, and with the others as they came along. He liked to be with them and never had any jealousy." Mary smiled. "I remember times in the early days before the others came when I was preparing meals. I'd bring James in by the hearth in his small cradle and Jesus would pull up his low chair and burble at him."

"Burble?"

"The stage before real words. But the eyes of James would light up and he'd wave his arms as though it were a conversation."

"Later on. In what ways was Jesus special?" Mark asked again. "Was it a particular quality that marked him as different from other children?"

"He was a very wise child from a young age. And his memory was amazing. He and his father worked together in the carpentry shop from—oh, he would go there from the time he began to walk. And as he grew in knowledge about carpentry he also grew in knowledge of scripture from the conversations they would have in the shop. The stories of our heroes, the prophets, the guidance of Moses. He learned from the Rabbi, too, of course. But his father was his real teacher. A patient, loving man.

"I remember one spring. Jesus must have been eight or so." She smiled at the recollection. "He simply could not understand King David and Bathsheba and David's sending her husband Uriah to the front of battle so he would be killed. He and Joseph talked about it for many days.

She laughed. "Oh, and the time when his father spoke of the kings of old and their wives. Jesus was intrigued, especially when he heard of Ahab's Jezebel and confrontation with the prophet Elijah. He asked his father at one point why he did not have more wives."

"More wives?" Mark asked, puzzled.

"Yes. Joseph had explained that the benefit of marriages to daughters of other kings created a web of alliances that prevented attacks by neighboring kingdoms. After digesting that conversation for several days, he asked his father about benefits our family might have if Joseph had one wife from a stonemason's family, another from the family of a man with large orchards, and yet another from an estate with large flocks of sheep. Joseph managed to assure him that one good wife was sufficient."

Mary's expression turned serious. "And Joseph taught all the children more recent history—about Judah Maccabee and the revolt against the Seleucid Empire and the rescue of the Temple from defilement.

"And in later years Jesus was schooled in other ways. I remember a terrible day when Joseph went to two fathers in the village whose sons had been taunting Simon, our youngest son. He had been lame from birth. Simon and the two other boys—all three must have been no more than six years in age at the time. They were on their way home from lessons with the Rabbi, and, oh, what they had learned that day!

"'Born of imperfection,' they cried, fingers pointing at Simon as other children came from side streets to see what the fuss was about. 'Child of sin!' Other words followed.

"Joseph, Jesus, and James were in the woodworking shop. They went to the door to peer out at the commotion, only to see poor Simon sobbing as he limped as fast as he could towards them.

"Jesus told me later how Joseph's face had turned dark red as he pulled Simon into the shop and turned on his tormentors and the children who had gathered behind them.

"'Go home, you idiots!' Joseph had shouted, pointing at the two taunting boys. 'I will come to see your fathers!' That evening he did so. He took along Jesus and the Rabbi, as witnesses.

"The story was all over the village the same evening. How Joseph and Jesus and the Rabbi had gone to meet the two fathers whose children had taunted our Simon. No pleasantries were exchanged.

"'Do you not remember my grandfather?' Joseph shouted in a voice that could be heard in the street. The two fathers nodded. 'Do you not remember my father?' They nodded again. 'And do you know me?' 'Oh, yes, of course,' they answered.

"'Let us speak clearly to each other. What sin did my grandfather or father commit, what sin have I committed, that can be said to have been visited upon my poor lame child?'

"'Joseph, Joseph,' one of the fathers replied, 'the games of children. What was said is unseemly but not to be taken seriously. Mere words!'

"'Words spoken with malice can pierce the heart deeper than the sharpest knife,' Joseph retorted. 'Shall our sons grow to manhood in this way?'

"They were silent, Jesus told me, casting glances at each other. Joseph's tirade continued. 'Yes, my youngest son has a lame leg since birth. How this has come upon him as his lot I do not know. But I wish him to grow and live in the spirit of the blessed Isaiah, Surely the Lord is my salvation. Therefore I will trust, and will not be afraid, for the Lord is my strength and my might.'

"Joseph then turned to the Rabbi. 'Rabbi, you and my son are my witnesses. Do either of you know or have you heard of any sin I have committed to cause the Lord to visit affliction upon my youngest son?'

"Jesus and the Rabbi spoke as one. 'No. None.'

"Joseph turned back to the two fathers.

"'The matter is settled. Let there be no more false accusations against my boy. Do we understand one another?' The two fathers nodded."

Mary smiled at the memory of the day long ago.

"And what did Jesus learn?" Barnabas asked softly.

"What did he learn?" Mary's smile vanished and her voice became fierce. "He learned that The Law and the Prophets are a guide and a guardian to the people of the Covenant, not an instrument for repression or ridicule. He learned by heart the words of the prophet Micah: 'What does the Lord require of you? To do justice, to love kindness, and to walk humbly with your God.'"

Mary fell silent. At last she raised her head. "It was not long after Joseph's death . . ." Her face lighted up with a lovely smile.

"Yes?" Mark prompted.

"He was healed. Simon was. Healed. He had been working in a field and fell ill. He was brought to the house unconscious with a high fever. I tried everything I knew to no avail. We kept vigil over him, and in the night Jesus took a turn. He was completely exhausted and half asleep when I relieved him and ordered him to bed.

"As the sun rose, Simon stirred and I felt his forehead. The fever was gone. I brought him some broth and told him to rest until the midday meal. We were gathering for it and Rebecca had gone to waken Jesus. Just then Simon, beaming with excitement, came through the doorway. He was walking without a limp!"

"God be praised!" murmured Barnabas.

"Once I was alone with Jesus I questioned him about what had happened during his time of vigil. He was puzzled at my question and told me he had said the prayer Joseph was accustomed to use when he sat with someone seriously ill. Nothing out of the ordinary, he told me.

"It was one more thing for me to ponder in my heart in those days."

ELEVEN

MARY SAT UP STRAIGHTER. "I could tell you many other stories. As Jesus grew into manhood he was known as 'the rabbi' because of his knowledge of God's way. Even our Nazareth Rabbi would consult him to resolve disputes in the community. What he learned came from Joseph and me, for we were at home with the scriptures. But his understanding went far beyond mere knowledge. It was as if the passion of Moses and the prophets dwelt in him and he often saw things through very different eyes than ours. And he also was a man of compassion who delighted in kindness. Surely you have heard how those closest to him described him."

"Peter told me of the Master's mercy toward him," acknowledged Mark. "Mary, you are angry with Peter's actions, yet Jesus forgave him. And after he told me, Peter burst out in laughter." He smiled at the recollection.

"When he quieted, Peter said to me, 'There we were, traipsing around the countryside with him. We were such knuckleheads! We could not see people as he saw them, especially the lowliest and the outcasts, as beloved sons and daughters of the Most High. We were dumbfounded when he spoke directly to women or touched lepers. Jesus, friend of tax collectors! He blithely ignored the Sabbath laws as though he were the Lord of the Sabbath. He told us of what was to come and we busied ourselves calculating who among us would have the most favored positions as though we were the guardians of God's rule.'

"Then Peter turned his eyes upon me." Soberly, Mark continued. "He said, 'You must tell of many things in your account, Mark.

But in them all you must be clear that Jesus was a man without guile, never calculating what would be to his advantage or gain. And when he was risen and instructing us, he kept reminding us, 'It is a new beginning for all people. God's Way.'"

Mary's eyes flashed with the anger that had mounted as Mark spoke.

"Perhaps I have erred about Peter. But I am no knucklehead and my hands are not rough from hauling nets and smelling of fish! My son was well educated and observant of the Law! I have not told you of the time our family and half the village journeyed south to Jerusalem for Passover. In the crowds and religious tumult we lost sight of our twelve-year-old. We thought he was with friends but he was not. He was missing on the way home so Joseph and I turned back to search for him." She held her head high. "And where did we find him? In the inner courtyard of the Temple, listening to the Elders and conversing with them about the Law and the Prophets! These stories of compassion for the lowly and the suffering! Even his brother James preached stricter adherence to the Law as the model for following Jesus' Way!"

"He followed God's Way," repeated Mark.

"God's Way," repeated Mary. "Yet terrible things continue to happen."

Mark frowned. His enthusiasm subsided and his voice was grave.

"Yes. Those who do such things have not yet heard the Good News. They do not yet understand there is a better way."

"Sinfulness and suffering will always be with us," she replied.

"But we have a choice," Barnabas protested. "The Master gives us that assurance. We need not always be caught up in a spiral of greed and hatred and retribution!"

"I am not as great a believer in good will as you and your cousin."

"But surely, you, his mother—"

Mary looked at both men with a level gaze. "Later in life I have learned to keep my thoughts to myself."

"But the Mother of Jesus?" exclaimed Mark. "Why do you not have a glad heart and rejoice in your son?"

The room was still as Mary's face reddened in anger. She turned her head away. At last she found composure enough to speak.

Twelve

"You were not present outside Jerusalem on that terrible day. What others did to him. What he chose to bring upon himself." Mary spoke the angry words slowly. "Yes, he was a man without guile. I wish he had had some."

She shuddered as though a winter breeze had passed through her.

"I *am* proud of him. A good son. A better salesman than his father with products from the shop. An understanding brother. A caring, compassionate man who would have been a wonderful father in his own time. But no, he chose another way."

Her eyes darkened. "He went to John at the Jordan. From there he walked into the wilderness. When at last he returned home he could scarcely stand. I fed him broth and washed him and put him to bed. He slept for days, his deep slumber broken only as I and his brothers and sisters awakened him for more broth. Late one afternoon when the others were at work elsewhere in the house or the shop, I was preparing soup in the kitchen when I heard a noise and turned. Jesus was limping to the table. He sat. He looked at me with eyes that glowed with passion and said, 'Mother, I know what I am to do.'

"He looked so weak and wretched! I held back my tears somehow and replied, 'Before you do anything you must gain back your strength.'

"Despite his condition he smiled at me. 'I love you, Mother. I need your help and then I will go.'"

Mary was calmer now. She fell quiet, her eyes moist. Mark and Barnabas said nothing, waiting for her to resume. At last she wiped her eyes with the tip of her apron and cleared her throat. She motioned to Mark.

"A cup of water, please."

When he returned with the water, she drank the cupful down and sighed.

"He remained with us for a time but took his meals separately. At the start he told the next oldest, James, that he was to remain in charge of the carpentry shop and construction opportunities. During the day he alternated between sitting in the garden and, as he grew stronger, walking in the countryside around Nazareth. It was in one of those walks that he learned of the arrest of his kinsman, John, taken from the banks of the Jordan to the fortress of Herod Antipas, who ruled Galilee and Perea after the death of his father, King Herod the Great.

"One day my son came to me and told me that he had arranged with the Rabbi to speak at the Sabbath Eve service. The time came and we all were in our seats at the Nazareth synagogue. The Rabbi introduced him. The passage for the day was from the scroll of the prophet Isaiah. Jesus was still quite thin but he read it out in a strong voice. I remember it still. She lifted her eyes to the ceiling and recited the words.

"'In the wilderness prepare the way of the Lord, make straight in the desert a highway for our God. Every valley shall be lifted up, and every mountain and hill be made low; the uneven ground shall become level, and the rough places a plain. Then the glory of the Lord shall be revealed, and all people shall see it together, for the mouth of the Lord has spoken.'"

Mary lowered her gaze. "Then he spoke of how other words of Isaiah now were fulfilled and all people were called to repent and to believe in the goodness and mercy of God.

"His teaching was well received and many smiles were directed at me. He was well liked in the community and there was much talk afterwards of the fame that would result for Nazareth from his homecoming.

"But it was not to be. Dark news of John's death came the very next day. Jesus was devastated. He withdrew into himself and spent several days in prayer, mourning the loss of his kinsman."

Mary paused. Mark and Barnabas were intently listening.

"He came to me at last and told me he was leaving. 'Stay longer,' I pleaded. 'You need more strength.'"

"'No,' he replied, 'it is time.'

"'Where will you go?' I asked as I held him close.

"He smiled. 'Mother, do not worry. I am going to speak to the fishmonger's widow, Mary of Magdala. She knows fishermen and others who will join me.'

"I was relieved. Mary was a friend. She had been through a dark period and half-crazed after her husband's death. My son had helped her to recover.

"And so, he went. That very day." She sighed. "But I made him promise that he would return before the next full moon. The son of a childhood friend of mine was to be married then. My friend and I had visited back and forth over the years. Her children were close in age to mine so they all had played together and were much like cousins as they grew older. My parents had died a short while before within weeks of one another and there was a new Rabbi in Cana. It was important for all my family to be there on such a significant occasion—the wedding in Cana."

Thirteen

"It was a lovely sunny day for a wedding. My friend was so glad we all were present. She had confided in me that her son was 'marrying up' to the daughter of a man with quite a large estate near Cana. The bride-price her son had paid was therefore nearly three times the usual amount and he had been quite concerned about the additional wedding costs. But he was to become deputy estate manager for the father, a widower, and his mother thought he could recoup his expenses in a fairly short time.

"The ceremony went well. The bride was beautiful; the groom was handsome.

"Afterwards we adjourned to the courtyard of the local inn. Long tables and benches were prepared for the bridal group and their guests. Jesus and I were seated across from the bridal couple at the center table along with the bride's father and other relatives of both families. The decorations were quite lovely and the requisite speeches were not overlong. After several toasts with wine Jesus and the groom began teasing each other about who had bested whom in games as they grew up. All in all, it was a very happy occasion.

"As I watched them, the words that Jesus had spoken in the Nazareth synagogue filled my heart, followed by a vivid memory of that day in the Cana garden so many years before and what the messenger had said: 'It is a new beginning.' And my son was conceived.

"I was pondering these things when the wine steward came and whispered to the groom. His face paled.

"Jesus spoke softly to him, although I could hear what was said. 'Is there a difficulty?'

"'We have finished the wine. There is no more.'

"Suddenly words came to me that I knew I was meant to speak, and I did so, in a low voice. 'Son, it is time for the new wine. The new beginning.'

"'Woman,' he answered, 'what has this to do with me?'

"I kept my voice low. 'It has everything to do with you. I know that now is the time. Your time.'

"He gave me a long, searching look, much as Joseph once had given me a long, searching look. Then he turned away. He reached across the table and put his hand over the hand of his friend. 'Do not fear,' he said softly. 'All will be fulfilled.'

"He lifted his hand and beckoned to the wine steward. 'Come closer.' The man leaned forward. My son nodded toward the tall stone jars at the side of the courtyard. 'Are those jars filled?'

"'No,' the steward replied, 'no ceremonies have been held here of late.'

"'Fill them with water.'

"'But, sir, for what purpose?'

"'Do as he tells you,' I said sternly."

Mary leaned back. She smiled.

"Have you never heard of that day? The wonderful day of lavish abundance of wine of excellent quality?"

"No," answered Mark, puzzled. "Where did it come from?"

"From the water jars, the water transformed to wine. They were the sign of the new beginning. He trusted me, you see. And he came to trust himself on that day."

Her smile turned to a frown and her eyes filled with tears.

"Which made what happened a short while later so very difficult."

Fourteen

"We did not see him for some time after the wedding. There were reports of his speaking in other synagogues. He had a band of fishermen with him by then. One of them was Simon, the one now called Peter. They were making their way through the northern towns and villages of Galilee. In periods when they rested, they returned to Simon's home in Capernaum because of Simon's concern for his mother. Simon's father had died and his mother had been ailing for some time."

She fell silent. At last she looked up.

"We heard that Jesus cured her."

"Yes," Mark responded quietly.

"I knew he would have no peace after that." Mary pulled her apron up to wipe her eyes. "When he came back from the wilderness he had unshakable convictions. I could tell he was on a path from which he would not be tempted. After the wedding in Cana he was sure it truly was his time."

She sighed. "He had the strength of will that Joseph often showed. And a stubborn streak inherited from me. He healed Simon Peter's mother and we heard reports of healings and exorcisms elsewhere. I knew it would lead to—to other things."

She paused, struggling with emotion. The two men were silent as they watched her.

"And it did."

She tugged her apron down.

"At first there were only a dozen or so who tagged along. Then more as word spread. Then still more until a great crowd followed him and his chosen disciples from village to village. Some in the crowd cried out for healing; others were watching to see how he did it, that they might do it also and have their own followers and acclaim. Such human folly!

"At every midday meal in our house we spoke of the latest stories that were reaching Nazareth. James was the most upset. He had had suspicions about the ambitions of our kinsman John. Now that John was gone he believed Jesus was following in John's path, speaking of a new baptism in the holy spirit of God. James was convinced that his brother's folly would lead to the same end as had befallen John.

"'He is crazed!' he exclaimed at one meal. 'One misstep and the crowd will turn on him and kill him! We must rescue him from himself.'

"I tried to reason with him, to no avail. From that day on, James delegated the carpentry work to his brothers while he roamed the countryside to learn when Jesus might be nearby.

"It was but a few weeks later that he reported that Jesus and those with him as disciples were returning to Simon's house in Capernaum.

"'Early in the morning we will all go,' he told us, his eyes afire with his determination to rescue Jesus, 'and we will force him to come home, if necessary.'

"The next day we made our way to Capernaum. My two daughters and I rode in the pony cart, with James handling the pony. Two of my sons rode our horse and the youngest son sat astride our donkey.

"We reached Capernaum just before midday. The lanes of the small fishing village were filled with people who pressed forward to the crowd milling about Simon's house. We tied our animals to a gatepost and pushed our way through the throng until we neared the front of the house. Its window shutters were open and we could hear my son's voice within. He was speaking about the love and mercy of God for all people.

"James slowly pushed his way to the door and spoke to a man standing there. The man nodded after receiving James' message and moved inside. There was a sudden hush within. Along with the throng we heard clearly the words, 'Your mother and your brothers and sisters are outside, asking for you.'

"There was a pause, followed by a low murmuring from inside the house. Then the voice of Jesus rang out: 'Who are my mother and brothers and sisters? Here are my brothers and sisters and mother! Truly I tell you, whoever does the will of God is my sister and brother and mother!'

"At once other voices rose in the house. Outside the throng pressed upon us, the men crying out, 'I am his brother,' and the women, 'I am his sister.'

"Angry eyes turned toward us, and we feared for our safety. The cries continued as we moved back through the crowd. My heart was pounding so hard and fast I feared I might faint. But at last we reached our animals. We were shaken, all but James, whose face was flushed with rage.

"'He is no longer my brother! From this day I curse him!'

"We made our way back to Nazareth in silence. I did not see my son again until the day another crowd pressed him forward through the streets of Jerusalem, a crown of thorns upon his head."

Her eyes moistened.

"Life holds such surprises. After the day of the horror on the hill, James later came to me and claimed that he had seen him again. He asked his brother for forgiveness and Jesus gladly gave it. Later James became a strong member of the Council in Jerusalem and was an advocate of the new Way, speaking in the courtyard of the Temple itself."

"I knew him then," murmured Barnabas. "Many people came to The Community in Jerusalem because of his strong proclamation."

Mark nodded. "He was tolerated at that time. Greeks and many other Gentiles became converts to the Jewish faith, and the religious authorities looked favorably on him."

"Until later years," added Barnabas. "When his preaching asserted that people of all nations are called to be God's light to the world."

Mary's face grew wet with tears. "And James, too, was killed. In a back street of Jerusalem."

Elizabeth stood in the doorway. "Have these men made you cry, Mother?"

"No, daughter. I was telling them about the time we went to Capernaum and the fierce anger of James."

"Old stories! 'We must live in the blessing of today.' Your words, Mother."

"Yes, my words. So many words."

Elizabeth spoke to Mark and Barnabas. "My mother should rest now. If you wish to speak with her further, tomorrow would be better."

They were reluctant to leave at such a point, but they nodded and slowly made their farewells and went.

Fifteen

THAT NIGHT TOO MANY memories aroused in the conversation of the day kept Mary from easy slumber. At last the cooler night air soothed her mind and she fell asleep.

She dreamed again of the holding pen and the white stallion.

The stallion stood at the center of the pen, his large eyes watching her as she approached the stonework.

"Why are you here?" she called out.

The stallion whinnied and shook his head from side to side several times and then was still.

She reached the stonework. She repeated her question.

The stallion whinnied again and stamped his right front hoof on the dirt surface of the pen. Once, twice, three times. He eyed her for a moment and then trotted nearer. She was fearful of the horse's intent, and she stepped away from the side of the pen.

The stallion paused. He turned his head and suddenly began to trot around the interior of the pen, following the circle of the stonework.

The trot became a gallop, faster and faster. The stallion seemed almost to whirl around the inside of the enclosure.

Mary was overcome with a sudden dizziness as she watched the horse circling past her again and again. She reached out her arms to the stonework for support and closed her eyes. It seemed as though the very earth on which she stood was whirling, faster and faster. Seven times the stallion circled.

The stallion stopped. The earth stilled. She opened her eyes and gasped at the sight she beheld.

No longer was the pen near the cottage of Amos and Rebecca. It resided on a vast plain, surrounded by ripening wheat as far as her eyes could see. The sun was behind her and its rays shone down and colored the stalks of wheat golden.

She looked at the horse. The stallion looked at her and whinnied. In the last moment before the dream vanished it seemed as though one eyelid closed and opened. The stallion winked at her.

Sixteen

THE NEXT DAY WAS sunny and pleasantly cool. Felix helped Elizabeth to move the table, benches, and an end chair for Barnabas outside to a level place near the woods. As the others gathered, Felix walked to the Lazarus chair at the end of the garden and sat in it. The sword in its sheath lay across his lap.

Mary stood by the table, facing Felix, her face flushed with anger.

"No, no," she cried out. "That chair is not for you!"

Startled, Felix rose to his feet and cast a questioning glance toward Mark and Barnabas.

"That is Joseph's chair!" exclaimed Mary. "It was his place at the head of the table."

"Mama, please," Elizabeth was waving a hand at her mother. "Lazarus also sat in it, do you not remember?"

"That was special, daughter. He was a comfort to me with his conversation."

Barnabas placed a hand on the chair at the other end of the table.

"I will give him this one," he offered.

"That is *my* chair," Mary stated. "I freely let you use it." She turned to face Felix. "But not that chair. It was for my husband only."

Elizabeth shook her head. "Mama, you make no sense." She extended a hand toward Felix. "He is protecting us from danger. He is our guardian, as Father was. Of course he is entitled to sit in a chair of honor!"

Mary gave her daughter a hard look that slowly softened as the others watched.

"Very well," she said as she gave a gesture in the direction of Felix. "He may sit."

Felix bowed to her and sat down as the others moved to the table.

Today Elizabeth sat alongside her mother on the bench, silent now but watchful as Mark and Barnabas took their accustomed places. Mark acknowledged Elizabeth's presence with a nod and turned his attention to Mary.

"I apologize for yesterday," he said. "I fear our conversation caused you considerable consternation."

Mary responded brusquely. "I am old. Sometimes I weep over things of the past. But they are gone and we must deal with present matters."

"I understand." Mark spoke cautiously. "But it would be helpful if we might speak of the incident in Capernaum once more. Briefly, of course," he added.

"Very well. Let us speak of it. Briefly."

Mark's right hand was sketching a circle on the tabletop.

"You loved your son. Yet he left you, a widow. He left his brothers and sisters bereft of direction. He left a thriving business. He left dozens if not hundreds of friends."

"As I have said, he was committed to the call of God."

"Yes. But you were angry yesterday when you told us about the incident and it seemed, forgive me but this is what I thought, it seemed as though you were glad for James' anger and cursing his brother."

"No. I hardly heard James' words. I was caught up in my own thoughts."

There was silence for a moment. Mark's hand continued to trace the circle round.

"Truth be, I was ashamed."

Mark's hand stopped and he looked at her stony face.

"Ashamed?"

"That my son who knew so much of scripture would dishonor his mother."

"But—" started Barnabas. Mark gave him a look and he fell silent. Mark nodded at Mary.

"Yes, to be the mother of a special son and then hear him say such hurtful words." He paused. "As we have talked together here, I have wondered whether those words truly are hurtful or whether they point us to our larger family."

"My family was quite large enough!"

"Of course," Mark soothed. "But what if the meaning of your son's words is to give you a much larger family, one made possible through his birth.'

Mary waved his remarks aside.

"There were other things he said and did with which I did not agree." Her words now tumbled out. "It was as though all the old ways and the history of our people and the holy covenant—none of them good enough anymore."

Barnabas could not contain himself.

"But it was—it is—a new beginning. As the messenger told you."

"I knew it would end badly. I had no inkling that it would be so terrible."

Barnabas protested, "It was through the awful day that you term 'the horror on the hill' that new life is possible! We need never fear death again."

"I do not fear death," Mary retorted and turned to face Barnabas. "I should have stayed with him. His disciple John pulled me away. I should have run to the watchers and begged them to kill me also."

"Mother." Elizabeth spoke softly and grasped her mother's hand in her own.

Mary went on. "I had already known shame before Capernaum. The betrothal—the day we went to Joseph's house. His mother's hissing. I was to be the object of contempt and ridicule. Only the trust of Joseph saved me. I am glad he died before he could hear the stinging words of Jesus."

"But the Master died so that we could have new life, as he does," exclaimed Barnabas. "Is this not important to you? The people he healed, the exorcisms, the teachings, all the words of hope and healing!"

Mark lifted a hand to silence Barnabas and addressed Mary.

"I hear behind your words a deep grief."

"It was a difficult time." She looked directly at Mark. "You were not there. Those of us who were there feared for our lives. I did not, but I knew I must see to my children's safety. 'Keep them from harm,' I told myself over and over in the days that followed."

Her tone became sarcastic. "But what did I hear from others? 'Ah,' I was told later during those days, 'we have seen the Lord.' Words from men whose knees had shaken in that room in Jerusalem. They would have turned shut a whole world of locks if the door had held them. Would the 'friend' who gave them use of the room betray them? Ha! None of them were prepared to die with their master! Cowards, all of them. *Not one man* dared to go to the tomb to perform the holy preparation rites for burial. *Not one!* And so the women who prepared their meals went. Such sacrilege! A shameful ending for the one who had called out in a loud voice, 'You are my brothers and sisters.'"

She fell silent.

Mark sighed. "It is all true. Yet it also is true that your son appeared to them and forgave them all."

Mary's eyes blazed at him. "So you persist in telling me. Has he appeared to you?"

"No, but—"

"What about the others? The ones closest to him? Did they see a restless spirit, as some Greeks believe?"

Barnabas spoke. "They affirmed it was not a spirit or some ghostly presence. It was the risen Master."

"I have felt his presence with me." Mark nodded at Barnabas. "And so has he."

"Is that sufficient?" she asked and looked at Barnabas. "The chair in which Felix sits is one in which our beloved friend Lazarus sat before he went to Cyprus. At times I can see the form of

Lazarus quite plainly until the morning sun rises higher. I have felt his presence with me. He has even spoken to me. Is this what you feel?"

Barnabas cleared his throat and spoke evenly.

"We do not believe in phantasms of the mind. It is much more definite than that."

Mary's mouth opened to reply but Barnabas raised his hand and she was silent. He continued.

"I myself was reluctant to believe. One day I was in Jerusalem for Shavuot, the day called Pentecost by the Greeks. Pilgrims were present from other places of Roman rule. I heard a man speaking in a Galilean accent in a nearby square. I could not quite make out the words and assumed he was preaching about the giving of the Law to Moses, a proper subject for the day. I drew near. It was Peter. He was speaking about the new life made possible through your son. As he spoke my heart was warmed and a sense of peace and wholeness filled me. I have never turned back to my old self since that day."

"I had such an experience also," Mark said quietly. "But it was not Peter who brought me to the Master but Paul."

Mary frowned. "The persecutor."

"Mama!" exclaimed Elizabeth.

"Yet your son forgave him." Mark said quietly.

"Yes, the world is quite turned upside down these days," retorted Mary. "But, please, tell me of the wisdom of Paul."

"It was not his wisdom but rather the teachings of Jesus he learned from the others during his time in the wilderness, before Peter became his advocate and Paul returned to Jerusalem and the Council. Where he received his commission to the Gentiles."

"World turned upside down," murmured Mary.

Mark ignored the murmur.

"Paul told me of teaching he held to be accurate and true. Stories of what your son taught the crowds around him. Taught them to think of a wholly new way of life. Taught them not to be imprisoned by the way things are but to receive God's freedom in the fullness of the Law. Freedom not to retaliate but rather to break the cycle of violence and retribution. Taught them love is stronger than hate. Taught them to help others to come to the light that overcomes darkness. Just as Ananias came to Paul in Damascus and brought his sight back to him."

"Yes, yes," Mary said. "I have heard of such things. Small good they did for my family!"

She glanced aside at Elizabeth.

"Jesus was to find good wives for my sons and good husbands for my daughters. He passed that responsibility to James."

"Mama, please."

"James had *his* awakening and remained in Jerusalem. No help from him. Rebecca was fortunate. She found the nephew of Lazarus pleasing and they married."

Elizabeth rose quickly from the bench in protest. "Mama, I am content to be with you."

Mary and the two men watched as she walked to the end of the garden.

Felix watched Elizabeth approach as she came near to him, but she shook her head and turned away to stare at the trees, her arms crossed upon her chest.

Mary sighed. "I have heard the talk of new relationships. The talk of a new world of being fully human and crossing boundaries. But what of his own family?" Her voice grew fierce. "Are we to be counted among the least? Supposedly the least are among the most blessed, but I feel no blessing, no blessing at all."

"Your blessing was to give birth," Mark said. "A new beginning."

Mary looked evenly at him. "A beginning of pain and families torn asunder."

"What do you wish from him?"

"I? I had dreams of my son becoming the greatest Rabbi of all. A greater teacher even than Gamaliel."

"And he is!" exclaimed Barnabas.

"So they say. Others."

Mark ran his fingers through his hair. "Woman, what do you want from him?"

"Nothing!"
"No, it cannot be. All this anger?"
Elizabeth spoke from the end of the garden.
"Tell them, Mama. Tell them of your heart's desire."

Seventeen

MARY TURNED HER HEAD to the house, her face stony.

Elizabeth took steps back toward the table.

"Tell them," Elizabeth repeated. "So that you may find peace at last."

There was silence save for a breeze that rippled the leaves of the trees in the wood as it passed.

"Holy Mother," began Mark.

"No!" Mary exclaimed, turning her face to him. "Only God is holy!"

She placed both hands on the table, pressing her palms down upon its unyielding surface. Her voice was fierce.

"My Joseph's favorite scripture in his older age was from the prophet Micah. 'What does the Lord require of you? To do justice, to love kindness, and to walk humbly with your God.' But my son, *my son*, has shown me neither justice nor kindness and God is an aloof stranger to me."

Barnabas, startled, "How can you say such a thing!"

Mary slapped the table with both hands. "I say it because it is true!"

With a rush of wings, the birds in the trees, startled by the commotion below, flew away.

Mark leaned back, eyeing her for a long moment.

"I think," he said at last, speaking softly, "I think you are not given the attention due the Mother of our Lord."

"Rubbish!"

"As you have told us, first you fell away from the gatherings of The Community. You were a woman known only as the Rabbi's daughter."

"For my own protection!"

"Perhaps at first. But all these years?"

"It is the wish of the Chief Elder. A man to be respected."

"And then," Mark continued, "you ceased attending the Sabbath services at the synagogue in Ephesus, where observance of the old ways gave you comfort."

"I grew old and tired of the journey. I observe the old ways here."

"You do not wish to be known as Holy Mother?"

Silence until Mark spoke again. "A woman to be recognized publicly and respected by all who follow the Way as the Mother of our Lord?"

Mary looked away. "Such things have no worth for me."

"The woman who served as an instrument of God for a new beginning, not just for the Jews but for all humanity. This has no worth for you?"

Silence.

Barnabas spoke. "Tell her."

Mark nodded. He spoke in a harder tone than before.

"In Ephesus there are households in which a silver statuette of you is enshrined. In the poorer households, one made of clay. In some households the silver or clay woman stands alongside one of Artemis. Is this pleasing to you?"

"It is of no importance to me."

"I find that difficult to believe."

Mary sighed. "They remain from the time of Paul's second visit." She looked at Barnabas. "The time when he wished to debate the High Priest of Artemis and you pulled Paul away to safety."

Barnabas nodded. "Yes. Many were unhappy because of the silversmiths who had turned to the Way and were now selling statuettes of you instead of Artemis."

"Mary," Mark spoke evenly, "the ones of which I speak are more recently made and sold. The Chief Elder is concerned."

"What has this to do with me?"

"Perhaps it is a comfort to you. Perhaps you have sent word to friends that such things give you pleasure. To be recognized as the Mother of God."

"No!" She slapped a hand on the table. "No! Graven images are forbidden! They are pagan!"

"It is not your wish or desire?"

"Oh, foolish, foolish men. I only wish to be recognized by my son!"

Barnabas spoke again. "But you are! He told you that he loved you!"

"Yes, and he spoke to me from the cross on that awful day." Her voice rose. "But not since!" Tears rolled down her face. "Not since. Not once."

Her hands covered her face as Elizabeth returned and placed an arm around Mary's shoulders. She gave Mark a fierce look.

"She is not able to reveal her true grief to you."

"I—I had no idea."

"You truly are foolish men. I will tell you, then."

She bent her face down and kissed her mother's hands, then stood again, keeping her arm around Mary.

"Mary Magdalene and Mary the mother of the other James, who became head of the Council in Jerusalem. What do they and others have in common?"

Silence except for Mary's weeping.

At last Barnabas replied. "The appearance of the Risen Lord."

"Yes. But Jesus did not appear to *her.*" Elizabeth spoke through clenched lips. "Nor to his other brothers and sisters. No vision of new life for *us.*"

"But surely your brother James—" protested Barnabas.

"Ha. James, the Righteous One, as he was called later, was too busy repenting daily of his former anger. The rest of us soon scattered in Galilee for fear of our own arrest and execution."

"Have you felt no warming of your spirit?"

"No. To hear you and others speak of such a thing only makes the cold stone in our hearts turn to ice."

"But your mother," sputtered Barnabas, "you and the others—for weeks before Shavuot the Master was teaching his disciples in Galilee by the sea. You could have sought him out!"

"Those first days we were intent on survival." She looked down at Mary's head.

"Mother was on her way with John to safety in Ephesus. James remained in Jerusalem. The rest of us quickly took what we could from the house in Nazareth and sought safety with friends in neighboring villages. Only later did we hear word from Mary Magdalene that our brother had been in the hills by the Sea of Galilee, teaching his disciples. Did it really happen? Or was it a rumor put about by his followers? By then he was nowhere to be found, and his closest followers were in Jerusalem."

"A very difficult time," murmured Mark.

"Lazarus came, still weakened." She looked around. "This house was purchased later by The Community as a secluded residence for Mother. At first Lazarus lived here as well. A neighbor down the hill, where my sister and family now live, prepared the meals." She gave a wintry smile. "Over my mother's objections.

"Lazarus sent word to his nephew that help was needed for a small farm, and when Amos came north he brought Rebecca and me with him. Amos purchased the cottage down the hill."

Mark spoke to Mary. "Was not Lazarus a comfort to your sorrow?"

Mary lifted her head. "He said only that Jesus would come to us. He was sure of it." She lifted the tip of her apron and wiped the tears from her face. "But my son never came. And Lazarus died a martyr in Cyprus."

"But you told us your youngest son is an Elder in the Damascus community. Surely he has found his peace?'

Elizabeth interrupted. "Have you seen the great statue of Artemis in all her multi-breasted golden splendor?"

"Only from the very bottom step of the temple," replied Barnabas. "Paul persisted in calling her 'Diana dropped from heaven.'"

"The Roman name," noted Mary's daughter. "But the cult of Artemis was strong here long before Rome."

"And it continues in strength," Barnabas noted.

"Yes. A small figure of a human woman, no goddess, was thought by many to be a fitting counter to the cult. A daily presence in a believer's home."

"Daughter," protested Mary, "stop! You must not speak of such things."

"They want the truth. If you will not tell it, I must."

Mary fell silent.

"During the second visit of Paul, John was gone and Paul stayed longer, teaching during the week and proclaiming the new Way at the Common Meal of Remembrance."

She glanced at the two men.

"As you have said, a number of silversmiths, Greeks, were taken by his words and joined the Community. They no longer formed the statuettes of Artemis for household worship and their families faced financial hardships. After much discussion among themselves they agreed it would be no sin to make a likeness of my mother."

"So we have heard," said Mark.

"Demetrius, head of the silversmiths, was incensed that the part paid to him from their former income had disappeared and he called the city to rally behind him on the day set for Paul's debate with the Chief Priest of the Temple of Artemis." Elizabeth looked at Barnabas. "You were there."

"Yes. There were thousands baying at Paul in the amphitheater. It was a narrow escape."

Elizabeth turned her gaze to Mark. "The public pressure was great. The rebel silversmiths withdrew from The Community and returned to Artemis. And that is how it continued until recently."

"So the Chief Elder has told us. Statuettes of Mary have returned in many homes."

"Yes." Elizabeth looked at Barnabas and again at Mark. "Let me describe what he has seen. An older woman in simple garb, hair covered, eyes downcast, with the sign of the Cross on the front of her cloak and her hands open to the viewer."

She paused. "Is this the image that the Chief Elder described?"

At the end of the garden, Felix rose from his chair and stood watching them.

"Yes," agreed Mark.

"I am responsible," Elizabeth said.

"You!" exclaimed Mark.

"Yes. The Community is larger now. It is a presence in the public affairs of the city. Many younger silversmiths are with us. My close friend Melina, wife of the silversmith Arsenius, knew of my concern for my mother. Arsenius made the design. Others helped in the manufacture."

Mary looked up at her daughter. "You were wrong to do this! It is a graven image!"

Her daughter smiled, "We are both worn down by the arguments we have had on this matter. But I believe it to be no graven image."

Elizabeth's voice rose. "What is the truth about the appearances of Jesus, my brother? Such a long time ago now, as you have said. In recent years I myself have found a way to come to terms with this hurtful neglect of his family. I have come to understand the truth of what you have said about the day in Capernaum. Through our brother we have become part of a family larger than our human minds can comprehend."

Mary broke in. "Daughter, please!"

Elizabeth lowered her voice and spoke tenderly, "It is an image of a real mother. Her hands have released her son to the world. I call it 'The Sending Mother.'"

"But this is—" began Barnabas.

"No," interrupted Elizabeth. "It is a sign of hope for all who believe, especially mothers whose sons and daughters follow Jesus my brother. You have been clear about the turbulent times in which we live. 'The Sending Mother' is reassurance that all will come round right in the end. This is the hope we hold dear."

"I do not agree with such folly," muttered Mary.

"I know," soothed her daughter, "I know. But I continue to be involved in The Community. I want to believe that my brother will come again. But these are difficult times."

Her gaze fixed on Mark. "I plead with you to seek an understanding for us with the Chief Elder. The statuettes are a holy reminder, not a profane symbol." She smiled down at her mother. "And they certainly are not a plea for adoration of, or veneration of, my mother. You have heard her thoughts on that notion."

Mary looked down at the table, her jaw clenched. No one spoke. At last Mark cleared his throat.

"I have heard the conviction in your voice. We need to think and pray about this matter," Mark said. "For myself I am concerned lest there be further division at a time when unity is essential. We will speak with the Chief Elder and other members of The Community. It may be a matter of days. With your consent we will return here to say farewell before travelling on to Antioch."

Mark rose. Barnabas followed.

"Of course," replied Mary.

Elizabeth took her mother's hand and spoke to the two men.

"I trust you will report to the Chief Elder the words I have spoken."

"Yes," said Mark. "We will lay the case you have made before him."

"Thank you."

"We thank you," Barnabas added, "for your hospitality. Know that we wish you and your mother well."

"Thank you," Elizabeth replied. "May you have safe travel."

Mary slowly rose and the two women stood by the table as Mark and Barnabas walked away to the path. There they hesitated, waiting as Felix assisted Elizabeth with returning the table and the benches to the house. When Felix joined them, Mark gave a final wave of farewell and they resumed their descent along the pathway to the house below.

Elizabeth put her arm around her mother's waist, watching the three men go. When they disappeared from view, Elizabeth and Mary turned and entered the cottage.

Eighteen

It was three days before Mark and Barnabas returned in the sunshine of early morning. This time they rode their horses slowly up the pathway. Felix was not with them. Once again the two sons of Amos and Rebecca preceded them, announcing loudly, "They're coming. They're coming."

Mary and Elizabeth were both at work in the garden. They stood up, watching the two men ride into the clearing.

"Good morning," called Mark as the horses halted. "May God's peace be with you."

"And also with you," the women replied.

"Will you have some refreshment?" asked Mary.

"Thank you, but no," replied Barnabas. "We are on our way to Antioch and hope to make a good distance by nightfall."

Mark nodded. "Once Barnabas and I reach Antioch, I hope to complete my account as quickly as possible. Copies will be sent to the larger Communities for their use. One will come to Ephesus."

He paused and looked directly at Mary.

"I appreciate what you have told me of the Master's conception and youth. These are important to our understanding of God's will."

He paused before continuing. "But I have decided that their inclusion in my account would be a distraction from the immediate call to faith for all followers at the present time."

He paused again and then nodded at the two women. "Mary, I have heard what you have said. I also have heard the conviction in your daughter's voice."

He smiled. "Elizabeth, despite objections from your mother, Barnabas and I believe your case for the silversmiths' work is a good one. The matter is not settled yet. The Chief Elder agreed that he will speak to you when there is some resolution. There is," he added, "considerable discussion under way in The Community."

"Ah," Mary muttered, "the Gentiles still win."

"The Lord wants us all to win," replied Barnabas. "Jew and Gentile."

"Hush, Mama." Elizabeth lifted her face and smiled up at the two men. "Thank you."

Barnabas spoke. "I doubt we will meet again, at least in this life. God be with you and give you true comfort in your son, our Lord."

Mark's gaze remained on Mary.

"In my travels I will persist in calling you Holy Mother, even though you do not wish it. You willingly became a chosen instrument of God for a new beginning. Remember the words of Lazarus and trust that you yet will see your son. And now, goodbye."

Mark and Barnabas turned their horses toward the pathway. Before their journey began, Mark turned his horse half round to speak once again to Mary.

"What you described of the wedding at Cana could be near the beginning of my account. It would follow the baptism of your son by John. And his time in the wilderness."

Mark continued earnestly. "But it is so different from the healings and teachings, I fear it would be a distraction. Perhaps another account in the years to come may include it. As for the incident in Capernaum . . . I agree with what Elizabeth said. Truly it marked a turning point in our understanding of God's will for all people."

He nodded. "Thank you again for all that you told us. Thank you for your hospitality and your patience with us."

He wheeled about. With final waves from the men on horseback to the women and boys gathered below their mounts, they were off.

Nineteen

Summer was followed by an unusually cool autumn and a cold winter. There frequently was snow on the hills north of Ephesus. As the seasons passed, from the south came news of the Great Revolt against Roman rule. Following the massacre by Jewish rebels of 6,000 soldiers of the Syrian Legion at Beth Horon, the Roman general Vespasian and his son Titus had been placed in charge. A new strategy was in place: eradicate rebel strongholds in the mountains of northern Galilee before marching on Jerusalem.

Mary was growing weaker; she now slept in the early afternoon as well as at night. Her energy and focus were drawing in. To accommodate her, the wedding of Elizabeth and Felix took place near the garden on a sunny morning in the spring. Friends from The Community brought food and wine for the wedding feast.

For the time being Elizabeth lived with Felix in his rooms at the Chief Elder's house. She had use of a horse and traveled up from Ephesus most weekdays to be with Mary. Rebecca and friends from The Community took the night watch and weekends.

The Community in the city continued to grow. Gentiles now far outnumbered Jews; the Chief Elder of Jewish background was succeeded by a Greek. A focus on Jesus the Master fostered a strong amity among all.

Visitors from The Community in Antioch arrived and introduced a new term, 'Christian,' for those who followed the Way of the Master, acclaimed as the Christ.

The completed Gospel of Mark was well received in Ephesus and elsewhere. Sections were read aloud throughout the seasons;

during the week of Passover Mark's Gospel was read serially, with the brief conclusion read at a special early morning service at dawn after the Sabbath. The baptism of new members followed.

Mary grew more and more weary. She sat in the Lazarus chair on the cool but sunny days and watched others deal with the garden. Her daughters fussed at her to eat more but Mary declined, saying she had little appetite. She became snappish at times, especially when Elizabeth hovered over her as she sat by the hearth in the small cottage.

A settlement had been reached about the statuettes. A compromise. Silversmiths who had been reduced to penury were to be allowed to manufacture The Sending Mother.

Visits to the cottage on the hillside by the new Chief Elder became more frequent. At one of them Mary told him during their conversation that she desired someone to come, someone with a good pen hand who could write down her wishes regarding her burial. Her desires were met. Thanassis came and inscribed her last wishes on a parchment of superior quality.

Twenty

It was autumn. She was surrounded by family and friends awaiting the end. Her children were there, along with the Chief Elder. Aquila and Priscilla, Felix and other members of The Community in Ephesus took turns in the vigil. Adam and Benjamin were solemn and required frequent hugs by Rebecca.

In midmorning Mary seemed to rally. She told Elizabeth expressly that she wanted to see the flowers in the garden once more. She tried to stand but could not. The issue was resolved after Rebecca tucked her back into bed. With Felix at the head and Amos at the foot, the bed was lifted and maneuvered through one door and then the outer door, finally to rest alongside the garden.

"Thank you," she murmured and turned her head to see the late-blooming flowers of autumn.

"It is a time for singing," declared her youngest son, who recently had become the Chief Elder in Damascus. His clear voice began a Psalm and the others joined in.

"I lift up my eyes to the hills—from where will my help come? My help comes from the Lord, who made heaven and earth. He will not let your foot be moved; he who keeps you will not slumber. He who keeps Israel will neither slumber nor sleep. The Lord is your keeper; the Lord is your shade at your right hand. The sun shall not strike you by day, nor the moon by night. The Lord will keep you from all evil; he will keep your life. The Lord will keep your going out and your coming in from this time on and forevermore."

They sang more Psalms. Aquila offered a prayer of thanksgiving for the life of Mary. Little Joseph and Judah told stories, memories from childhood, about their mother and father. As the morning passed into afternoon, Mary's breathing became a rasping gasp. "It will not be long now," noted the Chief Elder of Ephesus. "I will say the prayer." He lifted his hands upward and spoke. "Heavenly Father, our help in every time of trouble. May your great name be exalted and sanctified in the world, which you created according to your will. Establish your kingdom; may your Son, our Lord Jesus, be near. Receive now your servant Mary, blessed is she among women. May she hear your words of welcome, 'Come, O blessed faithful. Enter the joy of my heavenly home and rest from your labors.'" The Chief Elder paused and then said, "So be it, now and forevermore, as our Lord Jesus has assured us." The others gathered round said in unison, "Dominion and grace are with him; he makes peace in his highest heaven." The Chief Elder looked around the circle. "Now let us pray as our Lord has taught us: 'Our Father, who dwells in heaven . . .'"

Twenty-One

MARY DREAMED. ONCE MORE she stood by the pen, now residing on a vast fertile plain. There were neither hills nor valleys to be seen, only the ripening wheat from horizon to horizon.

It was midmorning and a bright sun warmed her back as she gazed at the white stallion.

The stallion whinnied a greeting and moved to the gate of the pen, around to the right.

Another whinny and the horse bent his head to knock against the gate before giving Mary a steady gaze. When she did not move, he bent his large head and again knocked against the gate.

It was a message. The stallion wanted out of the pen and only she could make it possible.

She walked around the arc of the stones and reached the gate. For a moment she and the stallion regarded one another. Another whinny came and she leaned forward and untied the coarse rope that held the gate shut. The gate swung open. The horse nodded his head and slowly walked past her into freedom.

She turned to look but the sun now was in her eyes. She sensed that she and the horse were not alone. Shielding her eyes with both hands she sought to see who stood there but the sun was too powerful. Its rays made her eyes tear up.

"Mother."

It was the voice of her son. She could not help but weep for joy, making her vision even more blurred.

"Oh, Jesus, my dearest! How I have longed for this day!"

"Come, Mother. We must go."

She felt strong hands at each side of her waist, and then she was lifted up and onto the stallion. In a swift move he also was up and seated behind her. He held her firmly from behind.

"Father Joseph, James, and Lazarus eagerly are waiting to greet you, along with a host of others. We will fly like the wind."

He laughed, a great gust of laughter, and they were off in a dash across the plain.

Epilogue

THANASSIS WRITES THIS AT my direction.

Upon my death I wish no ceremony other than the customary prayers. Bury my body in a simple shroud in an unmarked grave near the woods. Place the chair of Lazarus nearby.

I leave my house and belongings to my daughter, Elizabeth, and Felix, her husband. Should they continue to dwell in Ephesus and have no use for the house, it is to go to my daughter, Rebecca, and Amos, her husband, for their use. Should they not wish to hold the property, it is my express desire that the house be left open for nature to work upon it.

I charge the Chief Elder of The Community in Ephesus to proclaim at four successive Remembrance Meals that I wish no further rites at my grave, no veneration of any images that are alleged to represent me, and no use of any objects in worship that are contrary to faith in Jesus of Nazareth, my beloved son.

I further ask that this scroll be kept in safekeeping at the house of the Chief Elder with that of Mark's account.

May the words of the Prophet Micah be remembered forever: What does the Lord require of you but to do justice, love kindness, and to walk humbly with your God.

I ask forgiveness from the Most High for the times I have forgotten to live these words.

Signed by my own hand,
The Rabbi's Daughter

M